—*Just as the glow of the first cocktail cannot be repeated on any given party no matter how many may be imbibed, so the carefree days when the nerves were strong are gone forever for the man who has abused his nervous system through long periods of excessive indulgence. He has exhausted all but the most fleeting pleasures that can be derived from drinking, and he must understand that he can never recall them.—*

From page 72

—*There is so much excitement attached to alcohol, whereby the stupidest things become vitally interesting, that in moments of temporary sobriety the drunkard is apt to feel that nothing is of any consequence without it. He thinks that he has become so jaded that his power to enjoy simple pleasures, or even complicated ones, without artificial stimulation has gone forever.—*

From page 132

THE COMMON SENSE OF DRINKING

by

RICHARD R. PEABODY

1930

The Common Sense Of Drinking
Richard R. Peabody
1930

INTRODUCTION

In the twentieth century, with its high-pressure demands on nervous systems which have not yet become adapted to big business, mass production, telephones, automobiles, high economic standards—in fact, bigger, faster, and noisier living conditions—alcohol has come to play an ever-increasing part as a narcotic, rather than a mere social stimulant. Because so many can use it in moderation, and because of its social aspect, alcohol is seldom thought of as a drug—not, at least, until it has done its ruinous work on certain organisms that have proved unable to resist it.

I propose in this book to define the alcoholic, to show how he arrived at this condition, and by what method he may rid himself of his habit once and for all. While aimed primarily at the chronic inebriate the subject will, I think, be of interest to all who drink, more especially as it may show them where they stand on the line that separates moderation from excess.

Several years' experience in treating chronic alcoholism has shown me that it is perfectly possible to cultivate abstinence under certain conditions. It is a far easier task than the alcoholic has any idea of, provided that a scientific approach is made to the problem. Vague theories based on undirected will power are ineffective in the long run. Above all it must be remembered that eradication of the habit and temporary abstinence represent two totally different states of mind.

This book is in no way concerned with the arguments for and against Prohibition which roar louder and louder throughout the land. Needless to say, after ten years of the Volstead Act there still seem to be a great many men who are unable to regulate properly their consumption of the liquor they so easily obtain.

Drinking is a manifestation of the wish to escape from reality. The illusory charm of drink comes from the fact that the mental reactions to alcohol are extremely satisfying to certain basic psychological urges. Let any man reflect on his sensations subsequent to taking a drink and I think he will agree that the resultant feelings consist (1) of calmness, poise, and relaxation; (2) of self-satisfaction, self-confidence, and self-importance.

While the satisfaction of the demands for peace of mind and ego-maximation by alcohol may be legitimate for the average man who can control the use of it, certain individuals, normal in other ways, have an abnormal reaction to drinking. It is too fascinating to them. It poisons their nervous systems. Those who react in this manner must eliminate drink from their lives or suffer very serious consequences. If they are willing, these people can be shown how to train their minds so that they no longer wish to drink. They can learn to relax and to satisfy their egos in a manner that is constructive and permanent.

I have taken care to omit from my discussion all moralizing, knowing full well that the uncontrolled drinker is surfeited with it already, however true and justified it may be. He must be aware of all the reasons that his well-meaning friends and relatives have given him in regard to the harm that he is doing himself, to say nothing of his neglected obligations toward others.

Neither is the subject approached from the physiological side. Much authoritative information has already been written upon the destructive effects of alcohol on the bodily tissues. If these books should not be accessible to the individual seeking such information, a short conversation with a physician will shed sufficient light upon this important phase of the subject to leave no doubt in his mind of the harm that results from persistently subjecting the body to large and continuous doses of alcohol.

The explanation of excessive drinking lies in the field of abnormal psychology rather than in that of physiology or ethics. As a background to almost every case of chronic alcoholism there exists an inner nervous condition akin to the "unreasonable" feelings of anxiety and inferiority suffered by the abnormally nervous. It is precisely this condition of which moderate drinkers and other so-called normal people are fortunately unaware that makes hard and persistent drinking (on the part of those who cannot stand it) so incomprehensible. If friends and relatives wish to be of assistance, they must learn to realize that the nervous person with "imaginary" troubles is just as much in need of help as if he had an acute organic malady. Indeed, those who have experienced both forms of suffering would prefer to repeat the physical rather than the mental if they had to choose between the two evils. It is for the former alone, however, that they customarily receive sympathy.

The more the problem is imaginary, unreasonable, illogical, the harder it is to bear, because the individual suffering from it has neither the respect nor the sympathy of the outside world. What is worse, he has lost caste in his own eyes: he criticizes himself mercilessly, so that the resulting state of mind is one of fear and depression often bordering on terror. While the alcoholic in many cases may not seem to be deserving of pity, he nevertheless to some extent belongs to an unhappy class of neurotics, however much he may keep his mental discomfiture from the outside world or try to pretend to himself that he is free from it. It does him no good to be told that his troubles are his own fault and that all he has to do to get over them is to stop drinking. Though in a sense this may be true, it is of no help, because he is often motivated by inner forces of which he is unaware and over which, without scientific assistance, he has no sustained control.

The world is gradually coming to understand the importance of caring for the mind as intelligently as it does for the body, and that the pain resulting from a broken spirit should no more be faced courageously alone than that resulting from a broken leg. Yet what could be more indicative of a broken spirit than the perpetual attempt to escape from reality through excessive drinking?

Reality must be faced unaided by alcohol or any other drug. For the more responsible concerns of life, a state of mind wherein the individual actually does not want to drink must be attained. Such a possibility may seem so remote to a man who has been habitually drinking to excess that its mere suggestion is sufficient to make him shrug his shoulders in contemptuous skepticism, even though he would be free to admit that his present way of life is far from satisfactory. Yet it has been demonstrated over and over again that, in spite of the desires of the moment, sincere men and women anxious to work faithfully toward the goal of not drinking because they do not want to can create this relatively serene attitude of mind with far less hardship than they probably imagine.

—Contents—

III FIRST STEPS

IV THE CURE MADE EFFECTIVE

The Condition

I. The Personal Problem

Not long ago I interviewed a man who had decided that alcohol as a beverage had reduced him to a condition that lay somewhere between inefficiency and discontent, on the one hand, and potential ruination on the other. He could not confine his drinking to the occasion of which it was supposed to be a part, but continued it for at least one and often more successive days. In other words, he belonged to a class of people known as alcoholics.

Though emotionally out of hand, he was intellectually honest, and therefore he had no delusions as to his ability to confine his indulgence within normal time limits. One drink always led to another, and, what was far more serious, one night almost invariably led to another day. Every so often, medical intervention was necessary. He said to me, "I know I cannot stand alcohol. I must confess that an infrequent and short sojourn on the 'water wagon' is all that my efforts to control my habit amount to. I

1

have been admonished until I am sick of it, although what has been said to me is perfectly true and unquestionably deserved. Much of it has been said by people whose opinions I respect, people who in most instances themselves drink. While I have been severely criticized a few times, to be sure, I have as a rule met with more kindness than I have a right to expect. Furthermore, I have given myself many talks in the same vein which seem to me to be even better than those I have listened to. I have made resolutions not to drink at all as well as to drink with various limitations, but, except for an occasional month or fortnight spent 'on the wagon' in discontented sobriety, I never seem to get anywhere. Once I stayed on for six months, but I have never wanted to try to repeat the experience, if for no other reason than that I don't think I could. Needless to say, I fell off with a crash and started making up for lost time, though it had not been my original intention to do so."

Because he had ability as a salesman, a position which did not require daily attendance at the office, he kept his job. Because he was attractive, made money, and was always kind even under the effects of alcohol, he kept his wife. Because he was endowed with a strong physical constitution, he apparently kept his health. Nevertheless he unquestionably stated the truth when he said, "If I keep this life up much longer, I don't see how I can fail to lose everything."

This individual, while Intelligent and educated, is nevertheless a typical drunkard of the somewhat milder variety. He might drink even less and still be classed as a chronic alcoholic, but on the other hand he has by no means reached the lowest depths of disintegration as a result of his habit. While genuinely anxious to allay a condition that has become alarming, he does not in truth understand his present situation or its potentialities for the future, nor is he understood by his fellow beings. By his family, friends, and the public in general he is condemned out of hand as being a moral delinquent who could perfectly well control himself if he wanted to do so. In their criticism moderate drinkers, often show less sympathetic understanding of his condition than teetotalers. This the sufferer from alcoholism puts down as hypocrisy, when in reality it is misunderstanding. His actions are quite naturally considered at their face value without regard to inner impulses and their causes. "Why can't that fellow handle liquor the way I do?" is the comment of the normal drinker. "There is no need for anyone to make a fool of himself once he has had enough," he adds, and forthwith proceeds to instruct the alcoholic in how to drink moderately, not realizing that he is attempting to teach what can never be learned. Ignorance and good intentions often work closely together. The conduct of the alcoholic need not be condoned, but his personality and his problems must be understood if he is to be helped.

2. The "Alcoholic" Defined

What is a '"drunkard," "inebriate," or "alcoholic"? In the use of alcohol as a beverage there is a descending scale of mental as well as physical reaction, increasingly pathological, beginning with almost total abstinence and ending with delirium tremens, alcoholic dementia, and death. Just where on this scale chronic alcoholism begins is open to a variety of opinion, but for practical working purposes I draw the dividing line between those to whom a night's sleep habitually represents the end of an alcoholic occasion and those to whom it is only an unusually long period of abstention. The former class, which will be referred to as normal, includes the man who limits himself to a casual glass of beer, as well as the man who is intoxicated every evening. But at worst they are hard drinkers, going soberly about their business in the daytime, seeking escape from social rather than subjective suppressions, and to be definitely distinguished from the morning drinkers, who are, to all intents and purposes, chronic alcoholics, inebriates, or drunkards. There are normal men who occasionally indulge in a premeditated debauch, and who sometimes start the next day with a drink; but, by and large, the men who can drink and remain psychologically integrated avoid it the next day until evening (midday social events excepted).

More than one drunkard has told me that the first drink "the morning after'" was by all odds the best of all. They say it makes them feel as if they were coming back to life, as if they were no longer going crazy, and so forth. Such sentiments as these are absolutely incomprehensible to the normal drinker, to whom the idea of an "eye-opener" is almost always repulsive, no matter how much liquor he may have had before going to bed. I recognize, of course, that there is a small group of men who drink slowly and steadily day in and day out without any apparent psychic deterioration. Physically, they almost always break down in the long run, but, as this book does not deal with the physiological side of drinking, we shall disregard them except to say that their drinking is so methodical, their systems are so adapted to it, that as far as pleasure goes it does little more than bring them up to "par," actually a state somewhat below that in which they would be if they did not drink at all. If by chance they want to get a real "kick," they have to drink a prodigious quantity. Then there is a very much larger group than the one just referred to, who from time to time go on a premeditated spree, such as a class reunion or a New Year's week-end, and yet who by no stretch of the imagination can be considered alcoholics.

Lastly, there are a very few exceptions to the general rule who do take a drink the next morning to lessen the punishment resulting from a hard night, but who do not increase the dosage as time goes on. In spite of these exceptions, however, I think we may be justified in making the statement that those who can use alcohol successfully generally terminate the drinking of any particular occasion when they go to bed at night. On awakening, such sickness as alcohol may have caused them is of the body; their unimpaired nervous system sets up no cry for more. They are content to pay the price of their "good time" because the price is not unendurable; it has not changed much, if any, from their early drinking days.

But the drunkard with his nerves on edge is in a different plight. Once he has taken a drink he is quite rightly said to be "off again." When his friends are going to their offices, enduring such hangovers as they may have, he is back at the "speakeasy." If he appears at his work at all, it is only after he has been heavily "braced" to avoid the nervousness and depression of a "morning after," which he has become too cowardly to face. At lunch time he imbibes again to avoid the hardships of the afternoon. At five o'clock he can hardly wait to shake up his cocktails, and by late evening he is drunk again. Sooner or later, depending upon his particular stage of disintegration, he is unable to carry on his business at all until he has passed through a somewhat painful period of "drying out." Shortly after such a recovery the cycle recommences, with the alcoholic periods becoming longer and more intense. The resulting worry and feeling of guilt give the mind no rest when sober, in consequence of which these intervals become shorter and the nervous system receives no chance at all for recuperation. The victim is caught in an increasingly vicious circle. Drunkenness, acute nervous hangover, remorse, feelings of inferiority; then drunkenness again. A sanitarium may check temporarily the outward expression of this state of mind, but the inner urge continues to exist.

3. Types Of Drinkers

What sort of people reach this unfortunate condition and by what route? It is interesting — if somewhat disheartening for the purposes of determining causes—to note that the group which may be designated as "pathologically alcoholic" comprises persons from all walks of life, reared under the most varied conditions and undergoing the most diverse experiences. Racially, we might say that the Slavs, Teutons, and Anglo-Saxons are less able to control their consumption of alcohol than the Latins and Orientals, even though we should of course expect individual exceptions to the rule. Geographically, those living in the cooler climates seem more disposed to abuse liquor than those situated nearer the equator, though for some peculiar reason northerners who move south are apt to drink more than anybody else. The idea suggests itself that, inasmuch as drinking can be reduced to terms of nervous instability, it tends to be predominant among those who have a larger surplus of easily stimulated nervous energy and hence feel the need of something that in the last analysis soothes far more than it elates.

When we investigate any particular group, we find the most strikingly contrasted persons succumbing to excessive drinking. The rich and the poor, the highly intellectual and the ignorant, the frail and the robust, the shy and the apparently bold, the worried and the seemingly carefree, all furnish their quota of inebriates. We find that this unhappy group includes people of accomplishment as well as those who achieve nothing, the religious and the unbeliever, those with an interest in life and those without one, those who love and are loved, and those who are alone in the world. Among all these opposites and the many that come between we find a relatively small percentage, but a large actual number, whose nervous system cannot withstand alcohol in any quantity whatsoever.

While there are enough apparently confident and successful individuals who succumb to alcoholism to make impossible any hard and fast limitations to a particular type of personality, still the large majority of cases are found among those who are shy, egocentric, and shut in. Jung has designated these people as introverts. They are ably described by Dr. Abraham Myerson in his book, The Foundations of Personality:—

"There are relatively normal types of the heavy drinker—the socially minded and the hard manual worker. But there is a large group of those who find in alcohol a relief from the burden of their moods, who find in its real effect the release from inhibitions, a reason for drinking beyond the reach of reason . . .

"And so men with certain types of temperament, or with unhappy experiences, form the alcoholic habit because it gives them surcease from pain; it deals out to them, temporarily, a new world with happier mood, lessened tension, and greater success.

. . .

"Seeking relief from distressing thoughts and moods is perhaps one of the main causes of the narcotic habit. The feeling of inferiority, one of the most painful of mental conditions, is responsible for the use not only of alcohol but also of other drugs, such as cocaine, heroin, morphine, etc."

4. The Effect Of Inheritance

Unfortunately we can give no scientific explanation for the creation of alcoholics. Exceptions to any closed system of causal relationship would stare us in the face at every turn. The study of many inebriates, however, has given definite clues to certain features which have a distinct bearing on the majority of situations, so that within limits we can recognize the forces that have an influence on the shaping of an alcoholic career.

The first question to be considered is inheritance. To what extent are parents responsible for the development of this trait in their offspring through the transmission of the germ plasm? Without going into Statistics a cursory examination of this situation shows, first, that among the children of alcoholics there is seldom more than one in a family with this propensity. Secondly, that a much greater number have children who drink normally and in no sense as drunkards. Conversely, a great many alcoholics are born of parents who are temperate in their use of alcohol, in some cases being total abstainers. This would seem to indicate that a man does not acquire chronic alcoholism from his father or mother. Many inebriates use inheritance as an excuse, because it has become a sort of prejudice or credo to do so, but when they are carefully questioned they do not consider that they have any inborn taste or craving for liquor, once they have completely sobered up.

At all events, whatever the validity of inheritance as a cause, it has been definitely proved over and over again that it offers no insurmountable obstacle, or, for that matter, any additional impediment, to the overcoming of the habit once a man has definitely made up his mind to do so. What unquestionably is inherited is a nervous system which proves to be nonresistant to alcohol, though this same nervous system is more often acquired from neurotic parents who have expressed their nervousness in some other manner than that of chronic intoxication, just as a disposition to weak lungs is inherited and not tuberculosis itself, so I believe is a nervous system transmitted which is highly susceptible to alcohol and which may manifest itself in a variety of symptoms regardless of the original manner of expression. An investigation of the inheritance of alcoholics indicates in almost every case a neurotic history at least on one side of the family, and often to an extreme degree.

While parents may be exonerated as far as the direct inheritance of alcoholism is concerned, they cannot escape the blame for an injudicious early environment which they themselves have created. For many parents the bringing up of a child should require study and instruction from those who have made a business of treating children from the psychiatric point of view, particularly if the child presents difficult problems at an early age. Because a woman has had six or seven children does not mean that she has been an intelligent mother, as the lives of many members of large families bear witness. Mothers and fathers with the best intentions in the world can ruin a child's future because of a silly superstition that nature endowed all women, and some men, with a superior instinct for performing a very difficult task––namely, the efficient rearing of children.

I am reminded of Dr. Austin F. Riggs's statement in his book, Intelligent Living: —

"The relation of grown-ups to children is second to none in importance, whether the grown ups be parents, foster parents, or teachers. Obviously the future of civilization depends upon its children. The responsibility which they present to their parents and all other grown-ups is both immediate and absolutely non-transferable."

Certain features in the lives of many patients have stood out so clearly that it is pertinent to set forth what seem to be a few but indisputable instances of bad bringing up.

Too much prudishness and restraint either break a child's spirit so that he is never free from parental authority or, as a slightly better choice of two evils, drive him into open revolt. His mind must either become a vassal to that of his more dominating parent, or he must over assert himself to prevent this surrender. If to preserve his own personality he has been on the defensive with his family, he may in later life become unconsciously hostile to the restrictions of society without being in the least a misanthrope, and may feel that he is satisfying a morbid desire for self-assertion (freedom) by overindulgence in alcohol.

The spoiled child, on the other hand, receives no discipline at all, and so is unprepared to meet the world on anything like a give-and-take basis. Confronted with reality and finding it unfriendly compared to the unrestrained solicitude of his doting parents, he has a tendency to seek refuge in a parent substitute, something that will dull his hypersensitiveness and make him feel in harmony once more with an unsympathetic environment. It is for this reason that the majority of alcoholics are recruited from the ranks of only children and youngest sons. In his study, The Structure and Meaning of Psychoanalysis, Dr. William Healy makes an interesting observation.

"Rigel," he says, "makes much of a matter which comes frequently to the front in the modem child guidance clinic. He says that all sorts of considerations make it clear that normal psychic development depends upon the gradual emergence from a condition of parental authority. Failure in such a development will result in a relatively feeble adult personality. More dangers lie in the direction of too great rather than too little dependence on the efforts and guidance of the parents or their substitutes. However too sudden or too complete revolt from parental guidance and tradition may be productive of a bias against every kind of authority and convention."

Again, if the parents have been of equal influence and have taken opposite attitudes, or if the more influential has frequently changed his or her attitude, the individual grows up with a twofold ideal of self. He is of unstable temperament because he does not know whether to think of himself as a saint or a sinner, a success or a failure. One minute he has overconfidence and the next none at all. Now he may be elated for no particular reason, and now unduly depressed. These feelings may be semiconscious or they may be entirely unconscious and only demonstrate themselves in behavior. However, when confronted by situations calling for mature judgment or courage, a person brought up in the manner outlined is unequal to the occasion and, having already tasted alcohol as a matter of social custom, he flies to it as a refuge, knowing that for the time being he can have the courage and poise that he craves and that temporarily he will have compensation for his deficiencies.

Brutality, neglect, and the deliberate teaching of pernicious doctrines are so obviously detrimental to a child's welfare that they do not merit discussion. Rather, I shall conclude this all-important phase of parental influence by summoning to my argument four important quotations, the first two from Dr. Karl A. Menninger's The Human Mind and the latter two from Dr. Alfred Adler's Understanding Human Nature.

"The neurotic personality," says Menninger "is one whose primitive instincts have been modified to meet social demands only with painful difficulty. . . . This difficulty arises because of the prejudices, misapprehensions, shocks, rebukes, experiences, and parental examples of early childhood. Hence the neurotic personality is very definitely a product of

15

the childhood environment and depends largely on the individual's parents. . .

"The man was reliving a childhood situation in which fear had been instilled into him by an over-anxious fear-ridden mother, who robbed her son of his self-confidence. Or it may have been a hard-boiled, blustering, storming father, well-meaning perhaps, but intimidating. Some parents intimidate by silent disapproval, others by example, and still others by attack. Fears are educated into us, and can, if we wish, be educated out."

"It will be difficult," says Adler, "to mobilize a child who has grown up in a family where there has never been a proper development of the feeling of tenderness. His whole attitude in life will be a gesture of escape, and evasion of all love and tenderness. . . .

"Education accompanied by too much tenderness is as pernicious as education which proceeds without it. A pampered child, as much as a hated one, labors under great difficulties. Where it is instituted, a desire for tenderness arises which grows beyond all boundaries; the result is that a petted child binds himself to one or more persons and refuses to allow himself to be detached."

5. The Effect Of Environment

The temptation to drink, regardless of the parental attitude, does not appear as a problem until late in adolescence. At the earliest it comes up for consideration in the last year or two of school life, more generally upon arrival at college, or, for those who do not continue their education further, at the commencement of work. Obviously the family is still influential throughout the period which separates childhood from maturity, though as the boy grows older it is more and more modified by outside forces, sometimes in one direction and sometimes in another. These forces may be corrective or they may intensify the original trend. For instance, boarding school may give a child the assurance gained through relative independence that he could never have attained at home, or he may be overwhelmed by it through failing to survive among the fittest. For some, probably the large majority, boarding schools are of great benefit if for no other reason than that they remove boys from a too close contact with their families, but for the handicapped child who needs skillful Individual attention they are apt to be harmful. Schools differ so much, however, that it would probably be unfair to some to make sweeping statements about them as a class.

Just how much harm these schools can do in the

creation of alcoholics is a matter of varying opinion. My own theory is that in some of the most fashionable ones, where the discipline is apt to be of a severe order, a great deal is inadvertently done toward working up a thirst in the minds of the upper school so that, when left to themselves, they are more or less prepared to take up drinking as a serious business. This I think is due to two contributing causes. First, the discipline just mentioned is too confining, particularly as graduation approaches. The upper classes are not allowed much more leeway in choosing for themselves than the youngsters of the lower school. This results in an exaggerated sense of freedom upon arrival at college, a making up for lost time as it were. A superabundance of energy has resulted from the suppression of liberty with little experience in self-determination to control it. Secondly, there are the school graduates who return from the universities to see their younger brothers and friends in the classes one or two years behind them. From this source the schoolboys hear many lurid tales of dissipation, the suggestion being that the fast life is the one to lead and that anyone who objects to it is a "bluenose" whose opinion is not worth considering. It does not take much to make a boy of sixteen or seventeen feel that drinking is the smart thing to do. When a somewhat natural impression has been reinforced by the thrilling experiences of an "old grad" it is not hard to see what a boy's future aspirations will be when he once gets free from his preparatory-school confinement.

However, while this school life, with the graduate influence, is unquestionably a determinant in making a young man "hit things up" in the beginning, it is at its worst much more conducive to creating drinkers who eventually learn to control themselves than to the actual production of alcoholics. There are many forces working at this time, seemingly remote from alcoholism, which may be much more effective in producing that state than the gaudy tales of graduates. They are a part of growing up, and are independent of any single set of surroundings.

These are the successes and failures, the accomplishments and disappointments, of the young boy and adolescent. Are events shaping themselves in his life so that he becomes self-reliant and confident of his ability to mingle on an equal footing with his friends; or has failure in studies, in athletics, or in achieving reasonable popularity driven his thoughts inward so that he becomes shy, moody, or resentful at life?

While the major responsibility for an unsatisfactory adjustment lies in the atmosphere of the home during the first ten years, the next ten can do much toward the amelioration or elimination of it. A more careful study of the growing boy as an individual rather than as a relatively insignificant member of a group is almost as important as it was in the case of the child. In other words, if more individual psychology could be brought to bear in the formative years, the neurotic troubles of later life could probably be forestalled, in all but the most extreme cases.

Upon his entrance into the world, which takes place upon graduation from the secondary schools, the boy would find himself prepared to take up his responsibilities with mature judgment rather than with undirected emotions in control. In that provocative volume, Why We Misbehave, Dr. Schmalhausen remarks: On the high authority of Dr. William A. White, we are told that "many mental breakdowns, perhaps the majority of them, occur during adolescence or in early adulthood, and that systematic help extended to the youths in our schools and colleges would be of inestimable value in preventing such breakdowns."

Initial drinking generally takes place upon arrival at college. Now, whatever the prudes may think, a certain amount of drinking and even drunkenness at college is due to nothing more than a normal declaration of independence at coming of age, a youthful desire to be grown up, and an anxiety to be considered one of the boys. Most young men go through this stage none the worse for it, capable of taking up their responsibilities as they appear, with the drink problem well under control for the rest of their lives. In spite of spasmodic excesses they always have been and always will remain social drinkers, using alcohol as a stimulant to make a good time more enjoyable, and for the most part having the quantity consumed suitably adjusted to the occasion. To the truth of this statement the lives of the overwhelming majority of college graduates bear testimony.

On the other hand the individual of strong neurotic tendencies is undoubtedly weakened and prepared for a maladjusted life by a prolonged and intensive period of wild oats, whether the milieu be a college or a fast social set. Though he may show no signs at the time that he is to become a chronic alcoholic, subtle changes are taking place within him which may appear later in life. At an impressionable age he has formed a dangerous connection in his mind between happiness and rum. This criticism sums up the worst that can be said against the colleges; a not very damaging statement, when it is considered to how relatively few individuals it applies.

Most men are going to drink something and many of them a considerable quantity. The amount, so long as it remains within normal limits, may to

21

some extent depend upon the direct alcoholic suggestion received in one form or another. But the point I wish to make clear is this. Whether or not a man becomes an alcoholic as the term is defined in this book depends on character traits deeply rooted in his personality, and not primarily on exposure to an alcoholic environment.

6. The Attitude Of Mind

Such influences as I have mentioned are usually accompanied by an attitude of mind which more than any other factor changes the individual from a hard drinker into a true alcoholic. While this transition is often so gradual as to be scarcely noticed, I think, as I have said, that the decisive moment comes when a man finds out that a drink the next morning is soothing nerve medicine for the excesses of the night before.

I recall the case of a man who in his college days was faced with the problem of having to go to a lecture in an extremely nervous condition due to his drinking on many previous evenings. A graduate who happened to be in his club at the time asked him if he had anything to drink that morning. When told, "No," he evinced surprise that the boy should be willing to suffer "unnecessarily," and suggested to him that what he needed was a stiff drink of brandy to remove any unpleasant feelings of nervousness that he might experience during the lecture. This was a distasteful idea to the younger man, as it had never occurred to him before to drink medicinally. But rather than put up with his nerves any longer he gulped down what was offered to him. In the course of a few minutes alcohol had its narcotic effect and the lecture presented no difficulties whatsoever.

That drink was the beginning of the end for him, although he did not realize it until several years later. As he expressed it to me, "The handwriting was on the wall from that moment on, though of course I didn't realize it at the time." Then and there he conceived the idea that he could drink all he wanted to in the evening and take care of the resulting nervousness with a stiff bracer the next morning. For a year or two he stuck to his one drink in the morning after nights of excessive indulgence. But as he grew older, and his nerves were progressively weakened, additional drinks throughout the day became '"necessary," until he was having one every two or three hours. In a few more years he had reached the final stage of disintegration, where he would remain in an intoxicated condition for several days following a "party." He invariably thought that he was tapering off, but in reality he was gathering headway faster and faster, until he was drunk a large part of the time. Respites unfortunately only resulted in a physical recuperation that gave him the needed strength to repeat the performance.

After a period of sobriety the alcoholic wants his first drink for the same reason that his more moderate friends do—that is, to escape from reality. But in most cases he does not really want to continue drinking for the sole reason that prompted him to start in the beginning. Or perhaps it might be better to say that, while the same reason may be functioning to some extent, it is completely overshadowed by a greater one. He invariably claims that he is "easing" himself out of his condition, until he is entirely under the influence of drink again, and he is speaking the truth as far as his desires are concerned no matter how much his conduct and appearance may belie his statement. But he simply cannot stand the emotional disorganization that even a limited indulgence has created, and, although he realizes in the bottom of his heart that each drink is making matters worse, he postpones the ordeal of a hangover as long as he possibly can.

Are we to conclude from this that there is no such thing as the purely vicious alcoholic, that they one and all sincerely wish to recover from their habit? If we disregard the few moral delinquents whose mentality is practically psychotic,—that is, insane—and those whose failure in life has been so glaring that they are willing slowly to commit suicide, I think we might answer the question in the positive; the reason being that the genuine alcoholic, however he may twist and turn, is undergoing a very unhappy experience most of the time. His ethics may be nil, but he is getting so little out of life except downright suffering that he casts longing looks, not at abstinence to be sure, but at a successful career of hard but controlled drinking. As he can never attain this state again, whatever he may have been able to do in the past and no matter how hard he may try, and as he is unable even to visualize a life free from alcohol, he prefers what in his fatuousness he considers to be the lesser of two evils. To this extent only I think we may say that some drunkards wish to remain in their condition and refuse all offers of assistance which might show them a way out of it.

7. Danger Signals

From what has been said thus far it might be gathered that prolonged sprees lasting from two days to several weeks are the only form of drinking to be considered pathological and hence in need of formal curative measures. While this type of reaction is the most conspicuous, it is by no means the only manifestation of the fact that alcohol has disintegrated a man psychologically. In the first place there is the partial or potential drunkard who follows out the procedure of the individual outlined above part of the time, and the other part seems to drink in a fairly normal manner. If he is not slowly but surely increasing his dosage, he is at least rather uncertain of the outcome of any given alcoholic occasion, and as a result he keeps those who are dependent on him in a perpetual state of anxiety. His problem, if he wishes to stop his habit, is easier in one way than that of the out-and-out inebriate, because alcohol has not entirely absorbed his attention, but it is more difficult in another, because heroic measures do not seem to him to be so imperative and his tendency to rationalize on his ability to control himself has enough truth in it to prevent him from making a sincere effort. He is a drunkard every so often and a social drinker the rest of the time, but except as an aftermath of a disastrous occasion he bolsters up his self-esteem by thinking of himself as a social drinker, and it sometimes takes a genuine catastrophe to bring him to his senses.

Then there is the man who restricts his indulgence to the social event where it started, but who, during this time, runs amuck either habitually or at unexpected intervals. He may develop a maniacal viciousness which seriously menaces all who cross his path, or he may, with the best intentions in the world, perform insane acts which endanger himself and those about him. It is indeed far from unknown for an apparently mild person to commit a murder in a drunken rage without the slightest provocation, without, needless to say, premeditation, and without any remembrance of what he has done after he sobers up.

I knew a man who for no apparent reason developed a streak of madness while under the influence of alcohol which led him to run his horse full gallop at an eight-foot stone wall, killing the animal and all but killing himself. This extreme sort of behavior in certain individuals may occur regularly until death or the law intervenes, or it may come infrequently "out of the blue" as it were; in which case a certain amount of luck may permit the offender "to get away with it" for some time. As a matter of fact this horseman acted normally under the influence of drink a large proportion of the time, but occasionally he became temporarily insane, and at those times nobody knew what he would do—least of all himself. Alcoholic indulgence for this type of person is a more dangerous activity than it is for many out-and-out inebriates.

Of a similar nature, but to a modified degree, are the people who, while not actually dangerous, are morose, disagreeable, or disgusting, so that they make enemies, while drinking, through their slanderous remarks or vulgarity. As often as not these people are perfectly pleasant and gentlemanly when sober, though it is hard not to believe that there is a strong antisocial sentiment within them which comes to the surface when alcohol has removed the inhibitions. It behooves them not to irritate this abnormal streak, especially in a manner that makes them irresponsible when they are doing it. Many, though not all, of these obnoxious drinkers have considerable remorse when they sober up, particularly if they are confronted with and are about to suffer in some concrete manner from the harm that they have done. This naturally leads to brooding, an unhealthy activity for any mind, and such an unpleasant one that sooner or later alcohol in larger quantities is resorted to as a means of forgetting it.

While some degree of alcoholic depression following even a successful "party" is natural, a few carry it to an unwarranted extreme. These people are probably predisposed to a morbid state of mind in sobriety, and are living temporarily and in miniature what they may come to live permanently even to the point of a pernicious depression if they do not mend their ways. Their reaction to alcohol is a danger signal which should not go unheeded.

Unfortunately these various manifestations of drinking may be combined in the same man. At any rate those missing are in many instances latent and will probably develop under sufficient provocation. I knew an inebriate, whose conduct was for a long time condoned because of his humor and amiability, suddenly to become rude, obscene, and sometimes actively hostile. Another man with these unpleasant qualities to begin with always prided himself upon his ability to be at his office early the next morning in a state of sober efficiency. In the course of time he became a continuous drinker; he lost his habit of quick recovery, but he did not lose any of his disagreeable traits.

Once the nervous system has begun to react pathologically to liquor we can be sure of one thing only—it is going to maintain this form of "action", but in what way, and to what degree of intensity, time alone will tell.

Certain forms of conduct, as we have seen, are latent in the alcoholic, and we might suggest that they are latent in many more people than is realized. Whether such a manifestation eventually appears or not may be entirely fortuitous, depending upon the nervous strains to which the persons are subjected. The strongest systems have a limit to what they can withstand. A certain number, if hard enough pressed, will take refuge in excessive alcoholic indulgence, though they had for years thought of themselves as immune to abnormal drinking. Nor is it always disaster that produces the crisis. Success, particularly when it is financial, and thus permits a life of luxurious leisure, has been frequently known to create the same slavery to alcohol that is so often attributed to misfortune alone.

By this statement, however, I by no means imply that alcoholism is a probable or even possible outcome of the moderate drinking of the large majority. Far from it, as the life histories of an overwhelming number of men show. What I do mean is this—there are enough alcoholic breakdowns late in life to show us that there is a considerable group who only need a strong and easily accessible stimulation to force them from moderate drinking into chronic alcoholism.

II

DIAGNOSIS

1. A Typical Case

Bearing fully in mind the somewhat restricted picture that any particular case history can give of the whole problem, let us at this point sketch a typical alcoholic personality. This man, after thirty-six years of living and approximately sixteen of drinking, has definitely proved to his own conviction that he cannot use alcohol without abusing it, and that by his own efforts he is equally powerless to stop his indulgence.

While we need not discuss the characteristics of the grandparents, a short description of the father and mother will not be out of place. The father is a reserved sort of person with a keen mind, though shy, and given to mild periods of despondency due to a lack of success in a business to which he was never suited. His mother is domineering and prudish. He describes her as somewhat suspicious and fearful of the future, and he believes that she was mildly resentful of the quiet life which her marriage compelled her to lead, though she would never admit this and always referred to her husband in the highest terms. The family life centered about her. Our patient, in speaking of her attitude, says that she spoiled him in a negative sort of way—nagging him and making him think a great deal too much about himself. Everything seemed to be reduced to terms of right or wrong. Furthermore, he was made to feel in one way or another that the world was a difficult place to live in, and that nervousness was the rule rather than the exception. He thinks that the death of his older brother at an early age was partly responsible for her peculiar states of mind. Sometimes she had temper tantrums, which were apt to be directed at him if he were present. These were followed by remorse and a desire to compensate by being temporarily over solicitous. He never felt quite sure what her attitude was going to be, and, as his father considered it much easier to agree with whatever she said than to dispute it, he often felt very much misunderstood and friendless. However, he wishes me to understand that on the whole he received kind and generous treatment, and, while he does not look back on his childhood as something he would like to repeat, he does not feel that it was so very difficult.

Alcoholic drinks were served at the house as a matter of course, without any particular attitude being taken toward the subject. He does not consider that such drinking as he saw in his home has any bearing at all on his present problem.

His elementary schooling was completed without any occurrences worthy of comment having taken place. He went to boarding school, where he mixed well with the other boys; though he had a distinct feeling of inferiority which he thinks now came from being less mature as well as from a lack of ability in athletics. As he was small and not very strong, the others did not hold this against him, but nevertheless he was envious and admired greatly those who were more successful than he. There was little difficulty if any with the faculty, as his work was above the minimum required for passing and his conduct was somewhat better than the average, though he assures me that he was by no means a goody-goody.

There was no particular temptation to drink while at school. Three or four of his friends did so during the vacations, but it was so obviously done in an effort to be smart that he did not feel the least urge to imitate them.

In college his first two years were moderate in all directions, in spite of the freedom that he felt in getting away from school. His puritanical prejudices did not yield immediately to his newly acquired liberty. Furthermore he was not overburdened with money, and as a result he associated primarily with one or two rather conservative individuals who had been his intimates at school. He made friends easily despite his shyness. Eventually he joined a fraternity, and it was this influence more than any other that started him drinking. However, he does not hold his fraternity or the club system in general responsible, as there was no drinking allowed in the house and their were a few members at least who were total abstainers and more who drank in moderation. Nevertheless the friendships that he made at this time resulted in many trips to a neighboring small city, which invariably ended in drinking to excess.

At this point it might be well to state that he is not conscious of ever having had any trouble with his sex life. To be sure, the information he received on the subject from his family was scanty, but his friends supplied this deficiency rather adequately and in plenty of time to prevent any morbid introspection.

Of course at this period drinking did not seem to be any problem to him whatsoever. Custom soon adapted his physical system to it, and he had few hangovers. He maintained his ability to enjoy non-alcoholic occasions, though he noted a slightly progressive decline in this respect during his senior year. It was then, too, that he first began to experience nervousness; though on only one occasion did he notice the sedative effects of alcohol. This was inadvertent, a prolonged spree having been planned in advance to celebrate the end of examinations. It made a distinct impression on him, however ("that wonderful feeling," as he expressed it, "of being picked out of the depths so quickly in the morning"), but he did not deliberately use alcohol as medicine until some months later. He was in no sense an alcoholic at any time during his college career, nor was there any reason to believe from his conduct or from his mental attitude that he would ever become one. He said there were several boys who gave more evidence of becoming drunkards than he did, though as far as he knows only one lived up to expectations.

Upon graduation he enlisted in the aviation corps. He did not go overseas, but as he chose a particularly dangerous branch of the service he quite naturally had no feeling of inferiority in regard to his war record. He enjoyed flying and does not remember that he was ever particularly frightened by it. After fatal accidents, which happened often enough at the flying field, he became temporarily nervous and apprehensive, but to no greater extent than his brother officers. He thinks that his nerves suffered relatively little from his war-time experiences, but, as his excessive drinking began shortly after his discharge from the army, he is perfectly willing to admit that this may not be so. During this period he drank all that he could get his hands on, but except on one or two occasions this was never very much.

While in the service he married a girl to whom he had long been attached and who has since made him a very good wife, the only source of friction being his abnormal drinking. Even here he feels that she has been, to use his own words, "a damn good sport." An analysis of his married life seems to disclose nothing to excuse his exaggerated indulgence in alcohol. He thinks if he were single it would be worse, if that were possible.

After the war he moved to another city to enter a business that was soon to prove extremely successful. This gave him a superficial self-assurance which he unfortunately misused. Almost immediately he became associated with a "country club" crowd who spent most of their spare time drinking. While in the beginning he "carried" what he drank pretty well, he became increasingly nervous on the "morning after," and within a year of his discharge from the army he was bracing himself by pouring two fingers of gin into his coffee at breakfast. Furthermore he was sneaking additional drinks at the weekend parties—

a totally unnecessary performance, as almost all his friends were drinking openly a great deal more than they could hold. Sunday afternoons he generally became intoxicated again, and it was not long before he was decidedly under the influence of liquor from Friday night until Monday morning. This naturally required an additional dose of "medicine" to get him back to the office.

Soon he found that, if a drink at breakfast helped out the morning, another one at lunch saved the afternoon. So, slowly but surely, with infrequent periods on the wagon which were invariably terminated prematurely, he arrived at a state where one drink meant a two or three-day debauch. This would have cost him his job but for the leniency of his employer and his own ability as a salesman during his sober periods. I say "sober periods" because he felt that, while some business success could be attributed to artificial conviviality, he would have accomplished a great deal more in the long run if he had let the other fellow do all the drinking.

2. Self-analysis

Having ascertained in a preliminary interview that this man sincerely wanted to stop drinking once and for all, and would work seriously to that end, I asked him to set forth in writing his reasons for drinking.

Not being a student of abnormal psychology, he was not expected to unearth any hidden causes behind his reasons unless they came freely into his mind. His account of himself is interesting, however, as he was an intelligent person and, like the great majority of alcoholics, an honest thinker when sober. He was cautioned to avoid the petty excuses that all drinkers are wont to make in order to give themselves some flimsy moral justification. His short thesis on "The Causes, Reasons, and Excuses for My Drinking," as he entitled it, is quoted in full:—

"When I think of what liquor does to me and how much it makes me suffer, I sometimes feel as if I didn't know why I drank, as if any reason sounded too foolish to bother with. Then again when I concentrate on the problem it seems as if there were reasons or impulses, some of which are obvious, and some of which are vague and hence hard to explain.

In the first place my environment is a distinctly alcoholic one; even business seems to demand a certain amount of drinking, either to land a sale or to be congenial with the men in the office after hours. The country dub where my wife and I spend most of our spare time is of course wringing wet, and it seems as if I were forever expected to shake up a drink for someone else or that one was being shaken up for me. Of course I don't want to make a goat out of my environment. Only one of my intimate friends drinks as hard as I do and he is a rich bachelor, and many of them do not drink hard at all When it comes right down to it I have reached such a state now that I would probably try to drink all I could get in any environment.

When I start to sober up the next day I feel nervous and depressed, and I can't get it out of my head that one good drink won't set me up for the day the way it used to. So I take it and of course it doesn't, then I take another and the game starts all over again. I really don't want to stay drunk, whatever people may think; in fact I don't even feel that I am drinking in the same manner or for the same purpose that I do at the beginning of a party.

After I have been sober, say, for a week, a part of me seems to be trying to fool the other part, and I begin to think that the next time things are going to be different. Though I really know in my heart that this is not so, still I am fool enough to think that it is. If by any chance I do make a success of it, which is very rare, I use it as an excuse for the next three months, forgetting the hundreds of other times where my schemes and resolutions for "drinking like a gentleman" have come to naught. When I do stay off it, I become envious of those who are drinking, and that makes me cross. I don't say much of anything to them, because I wouldn't get away with it, but every so often I take it out on my wife, which makes me ashamed of myself

I hate to admit that I can't handle liquor the way my friends do and the way I used to be able to, and at times I will think up the queerest systems of reasoning rather than admit that I am licked.

Then my wife likes to go out or entertain at home, and I like it myself as long as I can drink. She does not see why I can't drink moderately and always suggests that I have a cocktail or two and stop there, which of course I never can do because all one drink does, is to make me want another.

Furthermore there are the celebrations which have to be taken care of, such as football games, weddings, ushers' dinners, class reunions, and so forth. Sometimes it seems as if every Saturday and holiday came under this head.

More and more lately I have been using it as a sort of refuge from worry and troubles in general. If the market goes down, or if I have to entertain someone who bores me, I take a few drinks to forget it. As a matter of fact I get bored more and more easily, whereas after a drink or two I enjoy everything and everybody.

I have no real interest outside of business and drinking. I don't mean by that I don't like my home, because I do and I would feel like hell if anything happened to my wife. Also I like golf, and fishing, and shooting, but when it comes right down to it I would rather sit around and drink with a congenial companion or two than anything I know.

While I have never tried to get away from a wet environment, still I feel sure if I did stop drinking and went anywhere else I would find practically no one my own age who was not drinking something, generally enough to make him feel pretty good, even though he might not be actually drunk. It's hard when you are bored without it, and you see everyone else doing it, not to say to yourself that you will just take one and that won't do you any harm, even though you secretly know it is a lie. As far as the next day goes that is different, nobody is doing it then and I get no support or sympathy, but I can't help going on.

Another reason that goes with my grouchiness, when I am sober and see others drinking, is that I feel sort of out of place, tongue-tied, too tired at times to compete with their alcoholic wit. I guess you would call it an inferiority complex, though perhaps I am not using those words correctly.

That seems to be about all the reasons I can think of now, though perhaps some others will come into my head later."

3. The Roots Of The Trouble

The individual described here is a fairly typical example of a man who, by his own admission, has passed through the different stages from normal drinking to habitual drunkenness, although he has not yet reached a state of complete demoralization, nor has he committed any act or reached a frame of mind which makes the prognosis for a cure unfavorable. He has already found out that he cannot learn to drink normally, because he has exhausted all known methods in an effort to control his habit, nor has he even been successful in keeping it within limits satisfactory to an extremely liberal, if not actually dissipated, social group. While he feels that no irreparable harm has been done so far, he is convinced that his habit is progressive, and that if he keeps it up he will be down and out within a very few years.

What does an examination of this man's history disclose? What does an analysis of the past show as a cause for his inability to drink as his friends do, and what prognosis may be made for the future? (Incidentally I should like to state that it is very unwise to make any prognosis whatsoever until at least two or three months of consultation have elapsed. "Hopeless cases" sometimes show remarkable aptitude in rehabilitating themselves, and "excellent prospects" fail to measure up to what is expected of them.)

The most marked feature of this situation is the comparative normalcy of this man's life. There have been no obvious reasons why he should be unable to control his drinking within reasonable social limitations. He has not had a hard time in the world, nor has he experienced any severe shocks; in fact there was almost nothing until the end of the war that might give an inkling of the deterioration that he was to undergo. However, bearing in mind what has already been said in regard to inheritance and early environment, an analysis of his family relationship may not leave us so much in the dark.

His father, it will be recalled, was a reserved type of man afflicted with moods of mild despondency. His mother was prudish, domineering, and subject to tantrums—symptoms of an attempt to cover up her pronounced fear of the world. The characteristics of both parents inclined the child toward self-consciousness, for children unwittingly absorb and reflect the attitudes of those who bring them up. How much of this parental influence was imparted through inheritance and how much through precept and suggestion we will leave to the "Inheritance School" and the "Environmentalists" to decide. At any rate a hypersensitive nervous constitution was inherited, and an unfavorable home atmosphere in the early years of the child's life combined to create a personality ill-adapted to facing life with stability. Of the two influences I believe that the environment plays a more important part; but, from whichever angle the subject is approached, the resulting character is the fault of the parents, though in our use of the word "fault" we do not wish to conjure up an ethical concept so much as one of ignorance and lack of self-control—an ignorance which would be less excusable nowadays, in the light of modern knowledge, than it was at the time of this man's childhood.

Our patient does not seem to recall very clearly his youthful mental reactions save a fear of his mother—not of being abused, but rather of being interfered with and misunderstood. Also he was in a continuous state of uncertainty as to what her attitude was going to be on any given question, and how soon it would change to the opposite for no apparent reason. He made a particular point of avoiding her whenever he had something that he especially wanted to do, for fear of being thwarted, though very often his desires were perfectly harmless and natural. He would sneak down the back stairs and hide in the cellar until she went out, so that she would not have an opportunity to spoil his plans, a performance in which it seemed to him she specialized. At other times he would run from the house yelling at the top of his lungs to drown out the sound of her voice should she attempt to recall him.

This man as a child was unquestionably stubborn, and his mother was not always at fault except in so far as her lack of tact and control was originally responsible for creating stubbornness in her offspring. Our patient had unconsciously to choose between becoming a timid mother's darling, completely surrendering his own personality, or putting up an exaggerated opposition. Of the two he unquestionably chose the wiser course, though as a result he has had an antagonistic attitude toward life in general ever since. In fact, a neurotic, whether his neurosis takes the form of alcoholism or not, is generally reacting to life as he formerly did to his immediate family when it comprised his entire world. Where this child-world was consistent, poised, and mature, where it demanded a system of conduct which was justified by its own example, we expect to find resulting personalities who can adjust themselves to an ever-changing environment without remaining fixated in or regressing to an infantile state the minute they are confronted with the complexities of life. Where we have a different kind of child-world we must be on the lookout for individuals who have never matured and who will be tempted to adapt themselves through a stimulant-depressant medium, or take refuge in some other form of neurotic behavior.

It was pointed out to this man that he probably grew up with a twofold conception of self, largely unconscious, to be sure, but which gave him a feeling of insecurity because of the changing mental states of superiority-inferiority which his mother's attitude had produced in him.

What else can we find in this life history that has contributed to an emotionally unstable condition? I say contributed, because we have already had the seeds of the trouble sown in childhood, and they only needed the benefit of certain experiences in college and the war to make them sprout and flourish. But I want to emphasize that unless the seed had been there, and by seed I mean a disposition to react neurotically to life, the condition would never have developed, as the overwhelming number of normal college graduates and war veterans bear witness.

It should be noted, parenthetically, that the attitude toward drinking in some of our colleges does not help matters for the nervously inclined individual. This attitude, though seldom openly expressed, seems to be that drinking should consist of a "party." In other words, if you drink at all, you are supposed to become intoxicated. One of my patients, a man who had graduated from one of our largest and most celebrated universities, told me that it was considered almost degenerate to take one or two drinks unless they consisted of beer. You were supposed to leave it alone entirely or make a thorough job of it. This point of view, it goes without saying, was as unsuited to an unstable personality as it was nonsensical from the point of view of logic. Had this boy grown up under Continental influences, his reaction to alcohol might have been very different; drink would probably have been an accessory to other interests and not an end in itself

To revert, however, to the case before us, we should observe the part played by aviation in the further weakening of our patient's nervous system. The war seems to have had a marked effect on the nerves of many men, including some who never saw the front-line trenches. "Shell-shock" often began its work on some organisms the minute they donned a uniform five thousand miles and many months away from the front. There were nervous breakdowns, in some cases reaching the point of suicide, on the part of men to whom the question, "Shall I be brave when the time comes?" occurred with morbid intensity even though it was doubtful if they would ever be put to the test. When this war state of mind was attained through aviation, it was increased a hundredfold, for an aviator did not have to go to the front to have his life in jeopardy a good proportion of the time. Few failed during their training course to see at least one, and sometimes many more, of their friends crash to the ground. Whether this fear of not being brave was conscious or whether it was largely repressed seems to have made little difference as regards its effect on the nervous system. In the case of our patient, while it cannot be considered as a fundamental cause of his intemperate conduct after the war, it most certainly precipitated matters. He undoubtedly would have been an unsuccessful drinker in the long run, but his army experience reduced the time limit by a considerable amount.

Another feature of military life that tended to make the soldier—and even a junior officer—irresponsible was the lack of initiative required in his daily life. The government told him what to wear, what to eat, and where and when to move about; in fact, his whole life was passed in carrying out carefully prescribed instructions. Superimposed upon this irresponsibility was an annoying confinement, so that when at last he was discharged it was not unlike being released from an honorable jail. The boarding school to-college change was in a sense repeated without the youthful nerves to withstand the shock, and, for an unfortunate few, without any increased maturity.

So, with his nerves frayed by aviation, with a feeling of escape from an absolute discipline, with a justified sense of having done his duty (and hence being entitled to allowances), and with a young wife anxious to have a good time, our patient found himself in a large city among strangers. There followed a period of business success, partly due to the intrinsic ability of the individual, partly due to post-war prosperity, and partly due to luck. The list of friends grew and the social demands kept pace; but the nervous system began to crack, and in order to keep it going, drink was used in larger and larger quantities as medicine. It was a social stimulant in the beginning, but, as hangovers could no longer be faced philosophically, a sedative was required to steady the jangling nerves. One had to work, one had to eat, and one had to sleep; drink unfortunately gave temporarily the strength on the one hand, and the relaxation on the other, to accomplish all these things. This man had in reality become a species of drug addict by carrying to excess a normal social custom. He would have been horrified at the idea of a hypodermic, yet alcohol had become a powerful narcotic for him without his having the slightest idea that he was an addict to any form of dope whatsoever.

4. Wine, Women, And Inferiority

In view of what has been said, it is clear, I think, that the real causative factors are those which induce a nervous condition first, and that this condition in turn induces alcoholism. In other words, alcoholism does not directly result from an event or a series of events in the manner that fever results from an infection. Drinking, or an isolated debauch, may follow a specific stimulation, but chronic alcoholism is a pathological method of life and not a mode of revenge, diversion, or even of suicide. The majority of men—and this must necessarily include a goodly number who are none too brave—simply do not choose that means of facing their troubles or of ending their life. Says Dr. Myerson in his Foundations of Personality: "Not all persons have a liability to the alcoholic habit. For most people, lack of real desire or pleasure prevented alcoholism. The majority of those who drank little or not at all were not in the least tempted by the drug. 'Will power' rarely had anything to do with their abstinence, and the complacency with which they held themselves up as an example to the drunken had all the flavor of Pharisecism. To some the taste is not pleasing; to others the immediate effects are so terrifying as automatically to shut off excess. Many people become dizzy or nauseated almost at once and even lose the power of locomotion or speech."

Anything that creates fear in a person creates uncertainty, timidity, inferiority; and so I firmly believe that the inferiority complex of the Adlerian School of abnormal psychology goes much further in explaining the origin of alcoholism than the pansexualism of Freud.

I agree with Dr. Schmalhausen when he says: "The ego is more pervasive as a human reality than sex. Human natures that harmonize on the ego level can contrive to put up with sex disharmony; but sex harmony cannot cope with the problem of disharmony rooted in maladjustment of egos. The Adlerian theme runs deeper in human life than the Freudian, though the latter, because of its dramatic and sensational components, gives the impression of being more fundamental."

Inasmuch as Dr. Schmalhausen's book, Why We Misbehave, is very far from being hostile to much that has been written by Freud, this remark is quite significant. At any rate I have yet to find a case of alcoholism which seemed to rest on suppressed sexual desires either normal or abnormal, unless all uncalled-for violence is to be interpreted as Sadism and all exaggerated friendliness is reduced to terms of homosexuality which does not seem reasonable to me. Nor does this opinion arise from any prejudice

51

against Freud in favor of Adler or from any a priori reasoning. As a matter of fact, it came somewhat as a surprise in my experience that alcoholics should be so free from sexual disturbances past and present.

As I do not explore the unconscious by psychoanalysis or hypnotism, I cannot make an unqualified statement that there is not a deep-seated relationship that can be discovered by these methods. It has, however, seemed unnecessary to go to such lengths to procure satisfactory results.

On the other hand, sex can function as a conscious or semiconscious stimulation to drink under certain conditions as contrasted with a fundamental instinctive urge. Men who are self-conscious in the presence of women find it easier to accomplish their purpose if their timidity is removed by alcohol (though "satyrs" never allow any blunting of their sensibilities to interfere with their pleasure). Furthermore, many men have more of a conscience than they realize. Alcohol will suppress this inhibiting force during the event and give them an excuse ("I wouldn't have done it if I hadn't been drunk") to dispel remorse after it is over. Thirdly, the crudities of course, inferior women are obliterated if men of sensibility drink a sufficient amount. Thus for many a bachelor, unable to find a woman of his own class, the old association of "wine, women, and song" consciously or unconsciously recommends itself.

For the man who is going to stop drinking, this association must be broken up. There is no biological urge for drink such as there is for sex, and only vicious custom has given them a connection. If this break cannot be made, then "women" must be avoided until the alcoholic habit has been definitely overcome. An inebriate's entire life depends on the successful outcome of the treatment; so it will not do him any harm if he finds he has to do without women until this has taken place.

In contrast to the sexual theme, their always appears inferiority in some form or another, often to a marked degree and in most cases fully admitted, although sometimes a compensatory mechanism is at work, disguised under a bold front. Alcohol, with the "Dutch courage" that it temporarily supplies, is a logical antidote for inferiority. Some of the causes of this inferiority, in addition to the early environment already referred to, are shocks, humiliations, accidents, failures in athletics and scholarships as well as in business, disappointments in love, inability to make friends, and the doing of some act which, even if unknown to the outside world, degrades the individual in his own eyes. According to Dr. Myerson, "Dutch courage" drove from many a man the inferiority and fear that plagued his soul. True, it drove him into a worse situation, but for a few moments he tasted something of the life that heroes and the great have. "If we can ever find something that does not degrade as it exalts, the entire world will rush to use it." *The italics are min*e.

A case might be mentioned of a man becoming a drunkard as a result, so he thought, of having his heart broken in a love affair. This individual had always been lacking in self-confidence, but his girl had temporarily given him the feeling of power that he had abnormally craved. When she terminated their relationship he collapsed. A short analysis soon showed him that it was his ego that was broken and not his heart. Sad he was, without question, but it was humiliation and not sorrow that "drove" him to excessive drinking.

Just as we speak of a vicious circle of cause and effect which moves faster and faster as drinking continues, so we can with equal validity refer, in the case of inebriates, to the cessation of drinking as a benign circle where confidence and poise follow sobriety, inferiority disappears, and so sobriety itself is made easier. Self-respect is substituted for degradation.

While the eliminating of drink itself has been the factor in determining this restored state of mind, still there may be other forces at work which determine whether or not the alcoholic is going to be able to complete satisfactorily his treatment. If he is leading, apart from his drinking, a life which causes him to lose caste in his own eyes, it is almost certain that he will conceive of himself as too weak or vicious to give up the drink habit, though this low opinion of himself may be partly repressed into the unconscious.

The most ready illustrations of the above condition are the sexual irregularities on the part of married men. Many men, as has been mentioned before, have more of a sex conscience than they realize. Some, of course, though they would collapse under the remorse following a petty theft and are in many other directions anything but conscienceless, have no immorality conscience at all. On the other hand, there are a great many men who pretend to this irresponsibility, whereas in reality they are unable to escape the traditions of their inheritance and bringing up. I have had two cases which have involved extramarital sexual relationships. In each case I replied that, as long as it did not lead to drinking directly through emotional contagion or indirectly through a feeling of guilt which produced inferiority, it was their own problem to decide. However, these men voluntarily came to the conclusion that, inasmuch as their wives were doing all that they could to make the home a happy one; they would make a clean sweep of their entire irregular life. They found that fundamentally they did feel conscience-stricken, and that in addition the fear of being caught had a demoralizing effect upon them.

I have known of other men in this predicament who, because of the difference of their natures, did not require the adjustment of this factor in their treatment and cure.

But sex is by no means the only cause for an enervating and demoralized self-ideal, nor is it necessarily the most important one. It was merely used as a convenient illustration. Any form of behavior which lowers a man in his own eyes, whether the outside world knows about it or not, will obviously prevent a vigorous, sustained, and undiverted concentration on the giving up of the alcoholic habit. Lying furnishes another excellent illustration of destructive conduct. A man who lies to those who have a right by nature of their position to know of his affairs is soon motivated by the feeling that if he is not man enough to tell the truth to those who are endeavoring to help him he is not man enough to give up drinking. While he may not consciously formulate this relationship in so many words, the effects—that is, his actions—soon testify to its validity. A man quite naturally has feelings of inferiority at the beginning of his treatment because of the effect that alcohol has had upon him, and so he should do all in his power to eliminate anything that fosters a lack of self-respect, whether it appears on the surface to pertain directly to the question of drinking or not.

"If," writes Professor McDougall in his Outline of Abnormal Psychology, "a unitary personality is to be achieved, the various sentiments must be brought into one system within which their impulses must be harmonized, each duly subordinate to the higher integration of which it becomes a member. This higher integration is what we call 'character'; it is achieved by the development of a master sentiment which dominates the whole system of sentiments, subordinating their impulses to its own. . . . The only sentiment which can adequately fulfill the function of dominating and harmonizing all other sentiments is the sentiment of self-regard, taking the form of a self-conscious devotion to an ideal of character. . . .

"A firm or strong or well-knit character, one that can resist all disintegrating influences, one that can face all problems, all critical alternatives, and can make a decision, can choose one of the alternatives and give that line of action an assured predominance over all others; and this capacity depends upon the organization of the sentiments in an ordered system dominated by a master sentiment; and of all possible master sentiments the most effective is a sentiment for an ideal of character, an autonomous self, a reflective self that can control, in the light of reason and moral principles, all the promptings of other sentiments as well as the crude urgings of instinct and appetite."

Another factor in the background of alcoholism, which is common to all neurotics, but which might escape those uninitiated to abnormal psychology, is the fact that by his conduct the alcoholic is making himself important in his own eyes. Prevented by his habit from living a constructive life, he is unconsciously anxious to make a stir in the world, even though this stir is of a purely destructive nature. Anything is better than oblivion, and so all the fuss that is made about him, as well as the fact that he is a "serious problem," is not as distasteful to him as he may imagine. In fact, he often considers himself a heroic villain or martyr. Those who have had dealings with drunkards have noticed the phase of self-pity wherein they expatiate at length about the curse that is laid upon them. They delight in relating how they are drinking themselves to death; it seems that they cannot help this unfortunate procedure, since, owing to inheritance or some other bugaboo, they are in the clutches of a "vice" which is more powerful than they are. Often this discourse is accompanied by drunken temperance lectures. In a weepy manner they implore their audience not to follow in their footsteps, and state with great emphasis that had they their lives to lead over again, they would never touch a drop. This is, of course, 100 per cent hocus-pocus, and nobody realizes it more than the man who has given up the habit "he couldn't help"' and has learned to satisfy his craving for attention in a legitimate manner.

5. Psychoanalysis

In the foregoing I have had occasion to refer to psychoanalysis. Owing to the profound influence that Freud and his followers have had on abnormal psychology and the justified interest that the public has taken in the popularization of his works, the relationship between this most important study of the human mind and alcoholism should be made clear.

When the large number of inebriates seeking help is contrasted with the relatively small amount of space that the psychoanalysts have devoted in their works to this phase of abnormal psychology, the thought occurs that possibly psychoanalytic procedure in this direction has not been as productive as it has been with hysteria, anxiety, and obsession neuroses. In Dr. William Healy's recent publication, The Structure and Meaning of Psychoanalysis, which Dr. Wittels of Vienna has referred to as a '"Bible of

Psychoanalysis," less than two pages out of 480 are devoted to alcoholism.

Nevertheless, since psychoanalysis has done more than anything else to illuminate for me the abnormal processes of the human mind, this form of treatment at the hands of an expert is most sincerely recommended when stringent methods seem necessary. I do not question the fact that the fundamental motivating cause of alcoholism may often be a conflict buried in the unconscious, but experience has shown others besides myself that methods more or less similar to those set forth in this book are in general adequate for cure without more intricate psychoanalytical investigation.

Of course I do not mean in the least to imply that exploration is neglected. The patient, as I have described, is encouraged to talk at length on every conceivable topic that interests him from his earliest childhood to the present time, and past as well as present problems are given special attention from the point of view of "confession" or catharsis. This, to many psychiatrists who are by no means inimical to psychoanalysis, constitutes sufficient analysis. Let me here refer to The Human Mind.

"One very useful method," (of treating nervous disorders) says Dr. Menninger, "is a combination of expression (analysis) and suppression (persuasion).

Sometimes it is called reeducation. It amounts to this. The physician learns as much as he can about his patient, in all the ways he can, but chiefly by as much mental catharsis and as much environmental investigation as possible. These he puts together, consults his knowledge of the principles of mental functioning and mental disease, and his experience with other cases; and on this basis he gives advice, adjuration, enlightenment, encouragement."

III
FIRST STEPS

1. Surrender

The first essential requirement for successful treatment is the sincere desire to be helped on the part of the alcoholic himself. Nothing constructive has ever been accomplished or ever will be with men who are dragged or pushed toward curative measures by friends or relatives. In fact, sometimes actual harm is done by such a procedure. A man will often reject premature persuasion, and, once having rejected it, may maintain his attitude for all time. He should be informed that professional assistance is available and then left undisturbed to seek it on his own initiative.

I can well understand from the point of view of the family that "premature" may hardly seem a suitable word to apply to a person who has been drinking to excess for many months and possibly years— but in spite of this fact, I repeat, he should be given the idea as a suggestion and then left alone to think it over. Nothing may ever come of it, to be sure, but on the other hand he may be much more concerned with the matter than appears on the surface. No action may result until some particularly depressing series of events has brought vividly home to him the futility of trying to continue drinking and the apparent impossibility of giving it up unaided. If he should have a friend who has been successfully treated and in whom he has confidence some pressure may be applied by this friend, but even here tact and suggestion should be relied on more than persuasion or exhortation. Alcoholics are apt to be extremely stubborn people; in fact, it might be said with much truth that the therapeutic problem consists in redirecting this stubbornness from destructive to constructive ends.

One man, who now no longer drinks anything, when first informed by an ex-alcoholic that there was a systematic method for treating inebriety, did nothing about it for a year, although it had long been obvious to even his most dissipated friends that he simply could not withstand alcohol. Matters naturally went from bad to worse, but this seemed to be necessary in order to convince him that his habit had definitely gotten the upper hand. When at last he awoke to his condition, he allowed his friend to bring him in for an interview. Before very long he was a successful case himself, though both he and the friend who introduced him had looked upon the situation as hopeless before the treatment. However, he did want to stop, or, to use his own phraseology, he "wanted to want to stop," which is all that can be desired in the uninitiated.

The surrender to the fact that alcohol can no longer be indulged in without bringing disastrous results is of such importance that it requires extremely thoughtful consideration. This surrender is an absolute starting point as far as the conscious mind is concerned. Experience has shown, however, that an intellectual surrender by no means settles the question, because there are unconscious motivations working in opposition which the patient must be made aware of and upon which he must devote considerable reflection in order that a distorted pride may be expelled from the deepest recesses of the mind. The alcoholic, in company with all other drinkers, started his habit with the idea of being smart or manly as one of the main impulses. Although this idea is supposed to pass away with the coming of maturity, in reality it does not do so. It still lingers in the unconscious as a sort of credo and accounts for much of the driving force which operates against a graceful surrender to the inevitable. In some cases it is fully conscious, and the individual frankly admits that he hates to say "no forever," for reasons which are hard for him to explain because they seem to be apart from an actual desire to drink. When he is confronted with the "manly" or "freshman" complex, as I often call it, a certain illumination is shed on the question, though often it takes a little analysis and planation for the idea to become a conviction. If he will face this problem and bring to bear on it the counter idea (which is, of course, only too obvious) that it is the manly thing to give up drinking because weaklings cannot do it, he will accomplish a great deal in the correcting of a very deep-seated obstruction to the cure. It is driving home platitudes as if they were profundities over and over again that actually unifies the emotional system with the intellect so that the latter has complete and permanent domination.

Another reason for not wanting to surrender is that the patient visualizes such a step in the light of an irrevocable pledge which he might someday want to retract. The sooner he takes this '"pledge" by himself, the better off he will be, but he is not asked to do so, and a little reflection should show him that as long as he remains in a civilized community there is nothing to prevent a retraction if he really wants to make it.

A third way of expressing this will-not-to-surrender is in terms of bogus freedom. The alcoholic wishes to feel "free" to do as he likes; he does not want to bow to the will of his family, his friends, the prohibitionists, or his own better self. This demand for free self-expression may be logical for the man who has drink under control. He may be justified in resenting the interference of those who wish by legislation to interfere with customs which are as old as civilization. But the drunkard should realize that he is in search of a larger freedom which rises far above the influence of man-made law. He has become a slave to something which can in the long run only be used by those who remain masters of it. In reality he has not known what freedom was since he first tried to limit his drinking and found himself unable to do so. The only freedom he can enjoy is that derived from an abstinence which gives him assurance and self-respect in his own eyes. When he knows each day what he has done, what he wants to do, and when he feels within himself the power to do it, then and then only can he understand the true meaning of the word "freedom," as well as the absolute bondage that he was in when he tried to express himself "freely" by drinking all the alcohol that he could lay his hands on.

These various theories for not surrendering are often supported by actions clearly showing unconscious motivation: such, for instance, as persistent attendance at very wet parties (though the patient was "absolutely sure of himself" before he went to them), quarrels with relatives and friends inducing self-pity, the distortion of theories designed for the elimination of drinking so that they come to permit of light drinking once in a while. This unconscious resistance against surrendering—that is, being cured is nowhere better demonstrated than by avoiding work and being late for or breaking appointments, apparently always with the best of reasons. There is a telling paragraph in Dr. Sigmund Freud's Introduction to Psychoanalysis: "If you were to come in contact with neurotics as a physician, you will soon cease to expect that those who complain most woefully of their illness are the ones who will oppose its therapy with the least resistance or who will welcome any help. On the contrary, you will readily understand that everything contributing to the advantage derived from the disease will strengthen the resistance to the suppression and heighten the difficulty of the therapy. We must also add another and later advantage to the gain of illness which is born with the symptom. If a psychic organization, such as this illness, has persisted for a long time, it finally behaves as an independent unit, it expresses something like self-preservation, attains a kind of modus vivendi between itself and other parts of psychic life, even those that are fundamentally hostile to it.'"

Of course a man cannot be expected to agree to do something until he knows of what it consists. Therefore one who has not been entirely convinced that he needs or wants help might be interested in a preliminary interview so that he can have first-hand information that may be of use to him some day, or that might entertain him as pure theory.

The attitude taken with such an individual is simply to answer his questions as fully as possible, discussing drink from any angle that he may wish. The accounts of changes in the lives of others more or less similarly situated may catch his attention and it may be possible thus inadvertently to "convert" him as to the advisability of seeking a cure. He is definitely informed that he is not interviewing an evangelist, so that whether he wants to stop drinking or not is most decidedly his own business. There is not the slightest desire or even willingness on my part to settle anybody's moral problems for them. If a person thinks he can drink, let him continue to do so. He may be right, and at any rate it is his own concern, whether he is or not. If his condition is extreme, not from the point of view of prudes, but from that of his drinking friends, and he does not wish to correct it, then he is either insane or a moral delinquent, in which case his problem belongs in another field.

When, however, a man is doing something that his more intelligent self (which he would like to have as a permanently directing force) knows to be the height of inexpediency; and when he admits, furthermore, that he can do relatively little about checking this something in spite of his desire to do so, then and then only is the prospect favorable. A person in the beginning cannot be expected to say that he wants to give up drinking in the broadest sense of the word, because if this were true he would promptly give it up without any difficulty and without any assistance, as obviously nobody compels him to drink. But on the other hand he can say that he would like to be shown how to reconstruct his mental processes so that in due time he will no longer want to drink. This is what I mean by the necessary "surrender."

2. Future Drinking

The patient's point of view in regard to future drinking is a second essential for successful treatment. He must have as his goal, no matter how fantastic the idea may seem in the beginning, the complete renunciation of the use of alcohol as a beverage in any quantity, however small for all time. No man who has ever passed from normal or hard drinking to chronic alcoholism, or who has shown persistently a disposition to act in an antisocial manner when under the influence of intoxicating beverages, can ever expect to be shown how to drink in a controlled manner, or to learn how by himself even after long periods of abstention. The very concept of eventual drinking, however remote, seems to be fatal to satisfactory results. The going-on-the-wagon point of view and the giving-it-up-forever point of view have little or no relationship. The first is only a stop-gap. Sober conduct, to be sure, may temporarily result from it, but the alcoholic conflict continues in the mind and sooner or later results in action.

Dr. Elwood Worcester, a pioneer in the psychological treatment of inebriates, tried in the early days of his work to teach drunkards to drink "like gentlemen." He told me that in spite of his best efforts he was 100 per cent unsuccessful. Because of Dr. Worcester's skill and experience this would seem to be convincing testimony of the futility of trying to teach the art of drinking to one who has ever reached the point where it has become a pathological problem. Mr. Courtenay Baylor, after seventeen years' successful work with alcoholics, is most emphatically of the same opinion.

Why it is that certain persons have a morbid reaction to alcohol after a period of fairly normal indulgence has been indicated in the first part of this book. Whether some day the microscope will disclose physiological deteriorations now unknown is a matter of mere conjecture. Nevertheless, lack of specific knowledge on this interesting point, however helpful it might be, does not seem to stand in the way of successful treatment. Once the mental conflicts, at least those within reach of the conscious mind, have been broken up, the outlook is forward rather than back. Suffice it to say—ONCE A DRUNKARD ALWAYS A DRUNKARD[1]—or a teetotaler! A fairly exhaustive inquiry has elicited no exceptions to this rule.

Of course a man who has had long periods of abstinence may on a few occasions be able to manage things pretty well when he resumes drinking, but sooner or later, depending some what on outside conditions, but still more on the stage of psychological deterioration that he has reached, he will crash harder than ever.

One of the reasons that may make it difficult for an inebriate to reform permanently is an idealization of the past, which he futilely believes he can revive, a belief often unexpressed with which he fools himself over and over again. "This time it is going to be different," you may hear him say, but if you know him well you will smile. There are plans made to drink slowly, to take small drinks, to stick to beer (the most futile of all), to prime first with olive oil, and not to drink before or after certain hours; all in the long run are of no avail. Then there are the occasions; at first only the big ones will cause the

---

1 Peabody was the first to state openly that once an alcoholic—always an alcoholic.

vows to be broken, but before long the little ones are getting their full share of alcoholic attention, and eventually they are deliberately invented. Just as the glow of the first cocktail cannot be repeated on any given party no matter how many may be imbibed, so the carefree days when the nerves were strong are gone forever for the man who has abused his nervous system through long periods of excessive indulgence. He has exhausted all but the most fleeting pleasures that can be derived from drinking, and he must understand that he can never recall them.

3. Economic Freedom

Some degree of economic freedom is necessary to assist in carrying out the cure. It is futile to attempt systematic character reorganization with a man who does not know where the next meal is coming from, or whether he is going to have a bed to sleep in that night. The idea of reform is obviously appropriate, but the development of the idea so that it becomes expressed in sustained action requires sufficient freedom from the basic demands of self-preservation to allow the drink problem, intrinsically so important in itself, not to appear to be relatively insignificant before the larger quest. It would seem as if destitution would act as a powerful deterrent to alcoholism, but, as is well known, the reverse is only too often the case when unstable personalities are involved. For this reason, among the poor only those who are at least assured of room and board while they are seeking employment are suitable subjects for reeducation. However, the rich and poor alike cannot await the ideal moment for taking up treatment, since it would doubtless never come. Many of the reasons why the present is unbearable for the alcoholic are derived directly from his drinking and will only be intensified by its continuance. Putting off treatment until this or that trouble disappears is just another way of saying one intends to continue. Experience has shown that the habit has been gotten rid of by many people whose lives were by no means a bed of roses at the time they started to work, but tended toward that ideal state in some degree when they took a mature attitude toward their self-improvement. If drink could permanently remove worry, most of the world would probably be more or less drunk a fair share of the time. But liquor as a diversion is definitely a two-edged sword, as the temporary oblivion gained from its use is unfortunately overcompensated for by an intensified and morbid remembrance when a state of sobriety is regained.

Incidentally, if a person is going to drink to any extent he should do so when he is in a happy frame of mind. The men who "get away with it" use alcohol in this manner because it does not require an increasing amount to make an environmental adjustment that is becoming more and more difficult. Some may claim that they know drunkards who only drink, or at least start drinking, in this manner—to celebrate rather than to seek refuge—and have the testimony of the drunkards themselves in support of their statement.

It seems hard to believe, however, that an otherwise sane person will deliberately ruin his life against his own best judgment for the sake of a most immature form of enjoyment unless he is motivated by a strong compelling force of which he is unaware and from which he is at times trying to escape. Because he picks his time for escaping at moments when his friends are celebrating, he is led to believe that he is doing as they are; but, with the full knowledge of his unfortunate reaction to alcohol, he would not attend these celebrations at all, or would not indulge if he did, if he were not motivated by an abnormal mental condition.

4. The Family

Unless a prospective patient is entirely on his own, a preliminary interview with his family or most intimate friend is most important. Much instructive material may be obtained from them which the patient cannot give, no matter how willing and honest he may be. Frequently what he says and does when drinking is a valuable source of information. The inhibitions are lowered and the resulting speech and action may show clearly the repressions, somewhat in the manner of a dream but without its symbolization.

Inasmuch as the family interview often takes place after the patient has been treated several times, it must be stated plainly that the latter's private affairs can be told to nobody without his express permission and that he is only being discussed for his own good. If this were not clearly understood, most people would disclose nothing of an intimate nature, and as a result the work would have to consist of persuasion devoid of analysis, with rather doubtful prospects of success.

Of even more importance than the information received are the suggestions which should be given the family to enable them to cooperate with the patient to the best advantage.

Another serious concern is the readjustment of the patient to his surroundings, of which the family is obviously the focal point. Where this is impossible, the surroundings themselves must be changed—a more difficult and less constructive performance, as it is often synonymous with hospitalization or permanent rustication in some remote spot. I am using the word "changed" in its most comprehensive sense minor changes in the environment are nearly always necessary, and generally the most important of these is the facing of the problem by the individual's family and intimate friends in an intelligent and cooperative manner.

In the first place, it must be understood that the immediate results of the treatment are far from satisfactory to the layman. There may be relapses throughout the first six months and sometimes these discouraging episodes are numerous and extreme. I say "discouraging" because that is the logical reaction of the uninitiated, but for those who have had experience with alcoholics these falls from grace are discounted in advance as being part of the normal procedure. In nearly every case the individual is slowly weaned from his habit. He is not instantly checked. During this weaning process the change in the fundamental attitude toward drink is often further advanced than would appear in actual conduct, though it is of course recognized that conduct in the long run is the only criterion.

In two extreme instances which I can recall no sustained progress was made during the first year of effort. Then suddenly both individuals completely eliminated their habit. As there was no sudden shock in either situation, the complete change of heart can only be explained on the grounds that the effects of the persuasion and the suggestion were accumulating in a mind that had been opened up by analysis, and when these suggestions became sufficiently strong the old habits yielded to them.

The first stage in the cure is reached when the patient abandons alcohol as a way of life, so that his upsets are actually mistakes and not a continuation of his former method of environmental adaptation. In the beginning the conduct itself may often be indistinguishable, but unless the patient is a liar (this trait is rare among alcoholics when they are sober, and when it exists the prognosis is very bad) it is easy enough to find out his fundamental attitude by asking him.

Relapses may continue after this important change has been made, but on recovery the patient reaches a different point of view: he has a sincere disgust at having been so stupid as to drink, a realization that the best part of his mind at least did not intend to do so, and a feeling that he got little or no satisfaction out of his "party" save in the early stages. Moreover, if with this new state of mind goes recognition that he has had long periods of contentment without recourse to alcohol, the temporary reversion to former conduct may be discounted.

But if after two or three months of work the patient feels that his basic attitude has not changed, that such temperance as he may have shown has been purely a matter of annoying restraint, then it would be worthwhile considering if a continuation of the treatment were warranted. This situation has not arisen yet.

What should be done with the liquor in the house is apt to be one of the first questions asked. The answer is that such dramatic gestures as pouring it away are futile. There is always plenty more obtainable around the corner. It is better to fight the battle out on the firing line, unless the patient definitely feels that it would be easier to have as dry surroundings as possible during the first part of his rehabilitation. If he does react in this manner he must say so frankly and without feelings of inferiority, for many first-class men have taken that attitude in the beginning, and it is only the stupid or insincere who force themselves beyond their limit. But most men prefer to continue serving their friends in the customary manner. They get a certain stimulating satisfaction in refraining from drinking when there is plenty of it under their noses. Best results are obtained, however, where this liquor is used in moderation as the sober view of "drunken parties" is apt to bore the non drinking alcoholic just as much as it does any other nonparticipant. As an escape from such boredom and as a result of concentrated negative suggestion the patient may be tempted to take refuge in the fatal "small one" as a means of adjusting himself to an annoying situation.

The inebriate who is attempting to overcome his habit must be given his way in regard to all things pertaining to an alcoholic environment. If he does not want liquor in the house, then obviously it should be removed. Furthermore, if he wishes to give up going to the houses of others, or to any function where it may be served and which would bore him when sober, then those who are primarily interested in him must arrange matters so that he has his way without making him feel that he is selfish and narrow. On the other hand, in this modern age, there is no reason why a wife who is well known in a community should not be free to enjoy herself as much as possible by carrying on her social life alone if necessary. Because the alcoholic chooses, perhaps wisely, to withdraw temporarily or even permanently from wet social functions, there is no reason for his becoming a dog in the manger. (Incidentally this is not a common trait in alcoholics when they have made up their minds to stop once and for all.) A woman may not want to leave her husband alone continually, but much of the time he should be glad to have her amuse herself in the manner to which she has been accustomed.

Whether a woman who drinks in moderation should become totally abstemious just because her husband cannot indulge himself without going to excess is a question to be decided on the merits of each particular case. A woman under the influence of liquor is naturally of no help to a man who is trying to give up the habit. On the other hand, the last thing that most inebriates desire is to feel that because they themselves cannot take one drink without eventually becoming saturated their wives must forgo such pleasure as can be derived from one or two cocktails. If a woman is actually dissipated she had better part company with her husband until he has had time to acquire a foundation of new habits. However, I have not yet known of a situation where a relapse was brought about because of a mild indulgence on the part of the wife.

While, as I have stated, the inebriate in process of reconstruction must unquestionably be yielded to in matters that immediately concern drink, he should not consider himself a hero and a martyr, and as a result use his praiseworthy efforts as a rod of iron with which to rule the home. Nor should he expect that just because he has stopped drinking everybody with whom he comes in contact is forthwith going to renounce all annoying traits and moods in deference to his change of heart. After all, he is only doing the sensible thing from which he himself will derive the most profit, and he must realize that his relatives' troubles and worries do not cease with his temperance, no matter how much his former course of conduct may have contributed to their aggravation.

On the other hand, the alcoholic should always be dealt with honestly, even when he is under the influence of liquor, as he is apt to remember a deception in a way that will react unfavorably upon those who are trying to help him, even though the latter may feel with justification that their relative or friend while drinking has no rights. For instance, if in order to get him home the alcoholic is told that he can have what he wants to drink when he gets there (provided he will stay there), then it should be given to him even if some friend has to go in search of another bottle. This arrangement, of course, could not go on forever, but a physician can generally induce sleep before the individual has gone much further in drunkenness.

I know of a case where an alcoholic went to an institution voluntarily on the condition that the doctor in charge would agree to his having four or five drinks on the day following his arrival and two or three the day after, a not unreasonable request. The doctor, however, deliberately broke his word. The result was that the cure of the patient, which eventually took place elsewhere, was indefinitely postponed because of the hostility engendered at what was justly considered the dishonest treatment received at the hospital.

5. The Patient

At the expense of some repetition, I wish to consider the treatment as it directly affects the patient.

The alcoholic is first shown that there are two types of men whose reaction to drink is so extreme, so abnormal, and so detrimental to themselves and to those about them that they cannot afford to indulge any longer in the habit unless they are willing to sacrifice their life to it. These types are the continuous drinker and the "bad actor."

The difference between the normal or hard drinker and the alcoholic is carefully described to the patient, as well as by what route the transformation between the two is made. The influence of inheritance and the influence of early environment on his nervous system are pointed out as being causative but by no means compulsive factors. He is told that practically every inebriate has had some such background as a cause of his trouble, and that if these were insurmountable obstacles to a cure, nobody would ever recover.

Then the patient is informed with all the emphasis that can be brought to bear that the sum total of experience to date has shown that if a man has ever definitely been unable to drink in a normal way (in using the word "normal" plenty of leeway is allowed for a good deal of dissipation) he can never again drink anything containing alcohol without the ultimate results being disastrous. He may do so "successfully" for a few times after long periods of abstinence, but there is a wealth of evidence to show that in the long run (and it may not be very long, either) he will become an addict again. If an individual insists that he is the exception to this rule, then the best thing for him to do is to go out and prove (or disprove) it, for there is nothing so convincing as personal experience, and there is very little use trying to persuade a man who has had an insufficient amount of it. If he is only a partial drunkard or an occasional malefactor, he will not be convinced that his problem is a vital one demanding solution unless he is unusually farsighted. The average man must learn the truth from his actions even though these actions may bring disaster in their wake. On the other hand, if a man is a definite alcoholic and yet will not admit that there is anything the matter, he is serving notice to the world to leave him alone, which is the only thing it can do until such time as his conduct necessitates incarceration—or he changes his mind.

Once the alcoholic takes up treatment, he must be absolutely honest in giving an account of his thoughts and actions, and he must take great precautions against lying ingeniously (rationalizing) to himself. "To be frank and honest in all relations," writes Professor Mc-Dougal, "but especially in all relations with oneself, is the first principle of mental hygiene."

A lie obviously does not hurt the instructor, but it creates such a conflict in the mind of the student that progress is at a standstill until it is uncovered. That a man will lie when drunk or when trying to sober up in order to get more liquor goes without saying. Furthermore, he may lie to his wife or to anyone else whom he fears, in order to cover his tracks and avoid a scene, but it is a very different thing to lie to the person who is treating the situation in a professional manner. As no promises are ever exacted, and as no one is ever ridiculed or scolded, there is no particular reason for untruthfulness save an unnecessary feeling of shame. If a person goes to a doctor with a pain in his stomach, he does not tell him that it is in his head if he wants to get well.

While on the subject of honesty we might mention that there seems to be a feeling among some people that secret drinking is a particularly reprehensible form of indulgence. As a matter of fact, if a drunkard is going to drink at all, there is nothing peculiar in his sneaking drinks in an environment which is naturally hostile. It shows rather more of a social consciousness than if he did blatantly what he knows is the part of folly. But on the other hand, where there seems to be no reason why a person should not drink in company and where he has plenty of opportunity to do so, then a preference to drink in solitude would probably indicate an abnormal personality.

6. Self Persuasion

A man must make up his mind to do everything in his power to cooperate in such work as there is to be done. Halfway measures are of no avail. Even if a patient is interviewed every day, it is obvious that one hour of instruction, analysis, and persuasion could not be effective should a man have an adverse or indifferent state of mind during the other twenty-three. He may listen dutifully while he is in the office and agree with what is being said to him, but if the subject leaves his mind until the next appointment, or if it is counterbalanced by destructive ideas which he could control, then his visits are doing him little good. An alcoholic should always realize that he himself does the actual work which produces the cure, though he may well need to be shown how to do it, and often be encouraged to carry it on. There is no wand to wave over his head wafting away by magic his undesirable habits. Two eminent Frenchmen, Dr. Dejerine and Dr. Gaukler, write thus of their patients: "We give them the desire to be cured, but it is they themselves who work the cure. This is the very thing which constitutes, we think, the great superiority of psychotherapeutic methods by persuasion. They develop in people the feeling of personality and responsibility, they increase their intellectual control, they accustom them to plan their lives and direct their energies by themselves."

The patient should view the process as he would a course, say, in medicine or technology. He knows perfectly well if he worked hard the first month or two at a medical school or engineering institute and loafed the rest of the time, or if he worked three days a week and knocked off for the other four, he would be neither a doctor nor an engineer, just because there are no lectures where attendance is taken, no laboratories where specimens can be looked at under a microscope, and no written examinations to be passed, the man who is going through a process of reeducation cannot afford to take his work lightly or informally. In reality he is undertaking the most important problem with which he has ever been faced, and unless it is solved in a satisfactory manner his life will be a total failure.

A man must be impressed with the fact that he is undergoing treatment for his own personal good and because he believes it to be the expedient thing to do. In other words, he is doing it selfishly as far as the guiding motive goes, though the results, if he is successful, will of course be anything but selfish. Others cannot help but profit by his change of conduct, and if that is the case, so much the better. But the minute a man seeks to reform for somebody else, no matter how deeply he may care for the other person, he is headed for failure in the long run. The old habits are for a long time trying hard to assert themselves, and as the work proceeds their attacks become more and more subtle. If he can lay the blame for failure at someone else's door, he will surely find a means of doing it.

Consider the case of a man who tried to give up drinking for the sake of a wife to whom he was most devoted. Drunk or sober, he was a very peaceable individual, but under special conditions these characteristics did not prevent him from picking an acrimonious argument with his wife one evening. When she quite naturally retaliated, he said, "All right! I've given up drinking for you and it's a damned hard thing to do, and now see how you treat me! I'll show you that I'm not going to stand for that sort of thing." He soon showed her by going out and getting drunk. As he had his pockets picked of two hundred dollars which he could ill afford to lose, he incidentally showed himself something, too. The motivating forces behind this performance were entirely unconscious, but when brought to his attention was readily admitted. He simply wanted to get drunk, but, as the old excuses about being cold and tired no longer held good, his unconscious invented what he thought at the time was a "real good reason."

The problem of drinking for the alcoholic is so important that it cannot afford to be contingent upon other people. If a man must avenge himself for real or imaginary wrongs, then there are plenty of ways for him to do so and still remain in a reasonably integrated state of mind. If, however, he takes a drink, he must realize that he is doing it solely because he wants to drink and not as a response to an external stimulation, whatever form this stimulation may take. The weather, physical fatigue, football games, New Year's Eve, and slumps in the market are typical "good" excuses. But, as I have said, the results of drinking are so disastrous for a chronic alcoholic that there can be no such thing as a good or bad excuse for drinking at all.

This, of course, means that an attitude of forethought must be maintained. Should the idea that the problem is after all not a vital one take root in the mind, the work might just as well be given up. The conviction of its supreme importance is an absolute necessity. The frequent inability to give up minor habits by those who have conquered alcohol is an excellent illustration of this point. By contrast the temptation is insignificant, but because these minor habits are very properly held to be relatively unimportant, no genuine sustained effort is put forth to suppress them.

Certain moments may be "seductive" if they are allowed to be, but the '"seduction" can be frustrated nine times out of ten by an advance mental preparation, and on the tenth (the unforeseen) occasion forceful common sense can be hastily summoned to a mind that has had methodical training in visualizing the problem in its true light. Because surroundings are highly respectable and the cocktail is very mild, the idea that "it won't do any harm to take it just this once," must not be allowed to take root in the mind for an instant. If this dangerous thought so much as shows itself, it must be swamped under an avalanche of positive suggestion.

The intellectual idea of abstinence is not of itself adequate to carry on the cure conscientiously over a sufficient period of time. It takes sustained effort to unite the intellectual concept which led the alcoholic to seek help with that consistent form of action which is an expression of an automatic attitude rather than a monument to will power.

Sound theory is an absolutely essential point of departure, but the statement that hell is paved with good intentions was never better applied than to the alcoholic who, almost more than anyone else, has become a specialist in avoiding life. Whatever may be the theoretical desire and intention, the old habits do not die as quickly or as easily as one could wish, nor are they dead and buried as soon as the patient considers them to be. In periods of emotional stimulation, whether pleasant or unpleasant, they may suddenly appear to the bewilderment of the person who had supposed himself to be cured "in record time." The habits of five, ten, and perhaps twenty years' standing are not going to pass out of the picture in as many days or even weeks, no matter how intelligent or conscientious a man may be in his application to the work. He has got to keep on directing his mental processes in a formal and definite manner for at least a year after his last debauch. The second year should be regarded as post-graduate work, during which the subject requires a modicum of attention. After that his new habits of thinking—that is, a genuine and automatic desire for abstinence—should have become permanent. But for the rest of his life he must allow himself just one thought in connection with drinking—under no circumstances can he ever drink anything intoxicating again. And "anything" most certainly must include light wine and beer; however harmless one may consider them to be.

A man will usually act according to his desires if it is possible for him to do so. Therefore my work is based on the idea that if a permanent cure for alcoholism is to be accomplished the mind must be trained so that in the course of time it ceases to want to drink. This for the drunkard, who has proved by his conduct that drinking is disastrous, is a normal goal which does not require any exotic ratiocination or mental gymnastics to be brought into harmony with logic. When it has been attained, he is no longer in a state of conflict, and his energies become released for other worthwhile interests and activities. This I think constitutes the all important difference between going on the wagon, even for long periods, and permanently effacing the mental attitude behind the habit.

A man who is on the wagon may be sober physically, but mentally he may be almost as alcohol-minded as if he were drunk. He is sorry for himself (a disastrous state of mind for anybody to be in) and he is envious of his drinking friends. He is constantly wondering if he cannot find an excuse for "falling off," and he is daydreaming of how happy and lucky he will be when the days of abstinence are finished. If he is not actually on the wagon, but is trying to curtail his drinking, he wastes his time attempting to devise various impossible schemes for making his drinking successful. Furthermore, he is doubtless depressed because of some fiasco that he has made of a recent party; he wonders why he did it, and whether he will do it again. He dreads what people are saying about him, and he knows in his heart, however much he may try to whoop up his courage by rationalization, that things are going from bad to worse. Nevertheless, life without liquor seems hopelessly stupid.

Looked at with a sense of relativity, to say nothing of a sense of humor, this is sorry stuff to obsess the mind of a supposedly mature man with normal obligations and responsibilities. Yet "obsession" is no exaggerated term to apply to the mental state of the individual who is trying to temporize with alcohol once he has exhibited a pathological reaction to it. Obsessions are arrived at generally after a long and intense application of erroneous thinking, and therefore it is no exaggeration to say that thoughts are most decidedly potent influences in determining people's lives. Constructive thinking must be stimulated in order that values be properly determined and desirable action set in motion. Therefore to prevent a continuous conflict, to prevent denial being a matter of will power, though power should be brought into play whenever logic will permit it.

Says Dr. Myerson, "Thought is powerful, words are powerful, if combined with appropriate action, and in their indirect effects. All our triumphs are thought and word products; so, too, are all our defeats."

Let the alcoholic, then, become accustomed to talking to himself in some such manner as this: "The most sensible part of me, the part that I consider my best self and should like therefore to think of as my directing force, does not want to drink anymore because much experimentation has proved it to be a most unsatisfactory way of living. Furthermore, it is my belief from what I know of the history of other alcoholics (whom I have no particular reason to believe differ materially from myself) that after a course of treatment, from which I learn in a scientific manner how to rid myself of the habit, I shall be very much happier than I can possibly be as long as I persist in trying to beat what has already beaten me soundly. Moreover, this satisfaction will be true from a purely selfish point of view, regardless of the happiness it may or may not bring into the lives of others. Of course I realize that there is a part of me, perhaps a large part in the beginning, that wants to drink. If this were not true it would be unnecessary for me to take formal action about it. But there is no use lying to myself any more or trying further to suppress my unfortunate desires in other words, pretending that this temptation does not exist. However, it does seem logical and reasonable to me that, if I really try consistently, I can reorient my opinion on the subject, which after all has been emotional, so that it coincides with my intelligence. This I have already admitted is the best part of me—the part which certainly should be in control of my destiny, and the part which secretly agrees with the world in thinking that I cannot and should not go on drinking."

This is the most important element in the work, the control and direction of the thoughts toward the ultimate logical goal. It is for this reason more than any other that treatment even with those whose theoretical desires (regardless of their conduct in the beginning) are sound must be patiently carried on over a long period of time—long, that is, by comparison with the time required for an intellectual under-standing of the treatment. It does little good for a man to endeavor to eliminate his habit until he con-siders it a sound, sensible, and desirable thing to do; something he would like to accomplish for his own sake, however difficult it may seem. Incidentally, for a man who is willing to buckle down to work the "difficulty" is always exaggerated in the beginning, as successful patients, without exception, have testified at the conclusion of the treatment.

On the positive side, then, the patient must keep before him the idea that his most mature intelligent self wants to stop drinking, and whenever he thinks of the subject he must drive this point home with as many reasons as he can muster from his experience to support it. On the negative side, all destructive daydreaming about the enjoyment of bygone par-ties as well as imaginary ones in the future must be checked as near its inception as possible. That these undesirable thoughts will appear, particularly in the beginning of the treatment, goes without saying, but if their presence prevented eventual cure no-body would ever get well. The all-important point is how they are to be treated when they do come to the mind.

The negative thoughts must be stopped, but the subject must not be repressed or even dropped from consciousness until it has been pursued to its logical conclusion with as many positive thoughts as possible. When at length the mind is diverted, the unconscious, which is supposed to retain all memories, must be left with a true picture of the whole situation and the individual's intellectual attitude toward it, so that it holds as a conclusion the idea that, whatever may have been done in the past, total abstinence is the only possible and hence desirable solution of the future.

The following example will clarify any doubt as to what is meant by the control and correction of stupid and dangerous reflections and imaginings.

A man who had successfully rid himself of alcoholism, and who had learned thoroughly how to guide his mind so as to maintain willingly his new attitude toward life, was walking along the street one spring evening. He heard a radio playing an old song which through association carried him back to his drinking days—in fact, to one particularly "glorious party." Before he realized what he was doing he had mentally relived the entire scene. But, even though cured, it would have been a mistake for him to leave his mind in this condition. Being aware of the danger of negative suggestion, he reviewed briefly his alcoholic history: all the trouble of which this party, among many others, had been the forerunner, and the recent debauches, with their painful recoveries––in other words, what a mess he had made of his life because of alcohol. Then he recounted how he had pulled himself together, just about in time, and how entirely different his life had become since he had given up drinking. By this procedure he overcame any tendency to action that might in the long run have resulted from his preliminary pleasant recollections. He had suppressed nothing, nor had he in any way lied to himself, but the final vivid impression left on his mind was that drink was something that he very definitely did not want to bother with again.

For emphasis I repeat; it is of supreme importance that positive thinking be employed whenever the subject comes up until the cure is complete, and that negative thinking be restricted to that small amount which automatically occupies the mind before the attention is aroused to combat it.

Negative thoughts, given the chance, arise all too swiftly. As the individual's adult life has been built around alcohol, it has naturally become an accompaniment to many of his instinctive urges––particularly his ego or will to-power urge, as has already been pointed out. It is his refuge in trouble and boredom as well as an apparent necessity at times of pleasurable excitement, because for the inebriate there is in reality little or no enjoyment without it. As soon as his intellectual control is shaken at all, and it takes very little to shake it, his emotions immediately take charge, which is almost the same as saying that alcohol takes charge, if there is any available. While in this condition he wants happiness and relaxation (of which I shall come to speak) and he wants them as soon as he can get them.

When treatment is under way, the patient is less liable to give in to these emotional states, as he has been forewarned of their probable appearance and has received instructions in handling them. Furthermore, he has taken a definite mental and a more matured emotional attitude toward them. This does not prevent, however, what are called conditioned reflexes—or, better, conditioned responses—from causing a certain amount of peculiar reactions until the mental processes are proof against them. Sometimes these stimuli are perfectly obvious, as would be the case when an alcoholic attends a wedding or dance or any other occasion where formerly he was accustomed to drink. But there are other unperceived stimulations which are connected in his mind with alcohol. When these are received by his senses, they may set in motion his former processes of thinking. Under this head might come certain faces, places, or sounds which are not consciously associated with dissipation although the relationship could be established if enough analytical association were employed.

The purpose of mentioning these conditioned responses is, first, to show why it is that a person who is trying his hardest to forget the subject of alcohol may so frequently think about it at unusual times; and, secondly, to explain certain annoying character traits which may crop out for apparently no reason, and which the patient in his bewilderment may at times think are almost as bad as the habit itself if they are to become permanent.

These traits are moodiness, depression, and sometimes anger, which apparently are without reasonable provocation. The inebriate misses his accustomed refuge, and furthermore he does not like to surrender to the fact that he must forgo what his friends apparently can indulge in. Moreover, he has in sobriety a surplus energy which he has been in the habit of deadening rather than utilizing. As nothing of a worth-while nature is at hand to which he can devote his attention the minute he sobers, up, the same discontent that he felt between parties is carried over into sobriety, but because he is no longer drugging himself he is more conscious of it. There is a feeling of emptiness and lack of accomplishment even though he may be rather proud of his ability to resist his temptation. Also, he is beginning to realize that this change might have been accomplished sooner, and that on the whole he has been stupid to insist on prolonging his excessive drinking until the last possible moment. Now these phenomena are sometimes entirely unconscious, and are activated to symbolic expression by seemingly irrelevant or insignificant events. That does not prevent them, however, from being a motivating force in the destruction of mental peace and emotional equability. The alcoholic must understand that the initial period of treatment is a transitory state, but that when his creative instinct is satisfied and he has had time to form new associations of ideas his negative moods will pass.

Parenthetically I should like to add that, if the patient has a tendency to be disagreeable while drinking, this will be intensified should he suffer a relapse. He will be conscious that he is doing something that he has taken very definite measures against, and that these measures were taken because his intellectual self had come to a realization that drinking for him was the height of inexpediency. This being the case, the alcoholic hates himself for his stupidity in a manner that he never did before he declared himself formally against the habit, and so in drunkenness this self-hatred is almost sure to be projected on to others.

One alcoholic found himself unreasonably disagreeable on returning from football games which he attended sober. It was the first autumn in many years that he had gone without liquor, and football had formerly furnished a particularly suitable excuse for intoxication. Apparently he thought little about his problem either during or after the games; in fact, he claimed to have enjoyed them almost as much as ever and he could think of no reason to account for his ill nature. Then he was shown that, inasmuch as he only began treatment in the middle of September, his old habit system, which he had not had time to eliminate, was still seeking its accustomed manner of expression. He was repressing this desire into the unconscious, and it was vicariously seeking satisfaction in the form of a temper outburst when he returned to his home. When this displacement of affect was analyzed, the after-game tantrums vanished.

While we have justly stressed the direct control of thinking and shown its supreme importance, we must add that such action is often best approached and accomplished by a combination of the direct with the indirect. The mind is never a vacuum—it is contemplating something at all times. Hence the elimination of an undesirable system of thought cannot be achieved alone by dwelling on the fact that such and such ideas (with their tendency to action) can be changed or kept out of the mind by concentration alone. The surest, as well as the easiest, way to keep the mind in a healthy state is to have it filled with constructive and diverting thoughts which occupy it because of their intrinsic interest and appeal. In other words, the sooner an alcoholic can become genuinely interested in some worth-while activity, the more of an outlet he will have for his creative urge, and hence the more easily he will rid himself of a bad habit without conscious effort. I have known of cases where men have accomplished their purpose without becoming interested in other phases of life until much later; but when a new interest can go hand in hand with the treatment the results of the work are quicker, surer, and more pleasurable.

There is so much excitement attached to alcohol, whereby the stupidest things become vitally interesting, that in moments of temporary sobriety the drunkard is apt to feel that nothing is of any consequence without it. He thinks that he has become so jaded that his power to enjoy simple pleasures, or even complicated ones, without artificial stimulation has gone forever. But this is true only temporarily. Quite naturally, upon first sobering up, the inebriate finds nothing in his life of constructive interest. Though his over stimulated imagination will put a damper on every idea in the beginning, he should give anything which may have a spark of attraction for him an honest trial. Time after time it has been shown that this interest achievement is no insurmountable task for a person of reasonable intelligence and the will to succeed. For instance, in the matter of conversation, the alcoholic will find that the same "intense philosophications" with which he was wont to bore bartenders and taxi drivers while amusing himself can in sobriety be carried on with people of his own level of intelligence; only, instead of nonsense repeated over and over again, they will become interesting and instructive exchanges of ideas.

Consider, for example, a young man whose chief interest in life was to become intoxicated and then discuss art, poetry, and literature with an equally drunken friend. He thought liquor and criticism were indivisible because without the former the discussion seemed to lack stimulation. Knowing that he had not taken the treatment seriously and would therefore again succumb to temptation, I dropped the hint that a review written under the influence of liquor (a time when he thought his mind was working exceptionally well) might be illuminating. The result was pathetic; in fact, so much so that I had difficulty in getting him to show it to me, although he was not as a rule a person who minded a laugh at his own expense. Then I persuaded him to do some literary work while sober, as he had a good mind and a keen critical sense. One night he undertook to write a thesis for one of those athletes who are too busy to perform such work for themselves. He started at 10 P.M. and it was 4 A.M. before it was completed and he realized the lateness of the hour. He said, '"For the first time in many months' " I was really taken out of myself mentally; for the first time since I began drinking I got a thrill out of life sober." This was for him an epoch-making discovery. Though very young, he was a real cynic; his cynicism was not a pose, as it is with so many young people. Therefore it was hard to convince him of the truth of anything that he had not himself experienced, and it was even harder to get him to experience anything in a state of sobriety. The effect of this writing can well be imagined.

There is in every man a disposition to create, and this disposition has the force of a fundamental instinct; whether its expression takes the form of painting pictures or selling bonds makes little difference so long as it brings satisfaction. When this creative urge, through laziness or inner conflict, is suppressed, it is bound to break out in some form of abnormal behavior. When a man is drunk, he somehow feels that he is expressing himself, regardless of how preposterous this feeling or its form of expression may be from the point of view of logic. The psychoneurosis, of which alcoholism is one manifestation, are often unsatisfactory substitutes for doing nothing or for perpetually doing something that is distasteful. (An exception to this statement is a person who has been doing something to his taste, but has been grossly overdoing it. This form of causation is, however, very rare indeed.) Thus it behooves the alcoholic who has been vividly demonstrating his discontent with life—or perhaps it would be better to say with himself—to seek a field of self-expression in which he may utilize his superabundant energy, which heretofore he had been drugging to the point of oblivion. Dr. William Healy writes: "Jung views the neurosis as the result of a lack of a positive goal or value in life and as really an attempt (unsuccessful) toward a new synthesis of life."

A debauch for the man who knows he cannot drink is nothing but an acute and vivid form of neurotic outbreak. While the satisfaction of this creative urge is most necessary for neurotics, it is particularly requisite for the alcoholic, because' contrary to opinion, he has in the majority of cases an unusual capability if he will avoid rum long enough to become acquainted with his own mind. If the energy and ingenuity that he has shown in becoming intoxicated are directed toward some more legitimate activity, he is more apt than not in the long run to go further than his sober competitor. In other words, his temperament is a powerful force for good or evil; it will take him far toward success and happiness, or it will consign him to hell.

The mind must be free of alcoholic doubts and conflicts, so that it can be devoted to the mature interests of life. There are different ways of freeing the mind, and it is important that the right one be selected. It has just been shown that an interest-diversion is most helpful in hastening and consolidating the cure, but the alcoholic must not become so absorbed in this interest that he forgets what actually is his main problem during the first year of treatment, a problem which before all else must be solved. Where drink is forgotten too soon because of its unimportance relative to something else,—a sound enough idea, to be sure,—it sooner or later returns to consciousness as being such a negligible factor that one or two drinks cannot make any difference. "Now that I have this new, interesting, and responsible position," says the pseudo-ex-alcoholic to himself, "I can handle the liquor problem in a normal manner. My energies are concentrated elsewhere, and my former reasons for excessive indulgence no longer exist." The only fault with this reasoning is that it does not result in either temperance or moderation, for when a drunkard resumes drinking it is never very long before alcohol again rules supreme.

Some years ago there lived a man who decided to give up drinking until he could make a million dollars, at which time he intended to drink in moderation. It took him five years of sobriety to make the million; then he began his "modcratc" drinking. In two or three years he lost all his money, and in another three he died of alcoholism.

The alcoholic, then, who is so fortunate as to have an absorbing interest during his period of reorganization must find time to carry on the work that is prescribed, otherwise his "old" habit will appear to him as something so far away and incapable of returning that it really makes no difference whether he has a small cocktail or not. So he invariably has one, and the results before long are in no way different than they were before he took up his new interest.

IV
The Cure Made Effective

I. The Mind

We have seen that alcoholism and the psycho-neuroses have for the most part the same fundamental bases though alcoholism is a rather more natural form of symptomatic behavior because of the social approval that accompanies moderate drinking. It is not surprising that what has been a social custom throughout history in all parts of the civilized world should be the natural method of relief for those of an unstable nervous condition who unwittingly crave a narcotic, but who are unfortunately unable to withstand its soothing influence. Because drinking alcoholic beverages is considered to be normal up to a certain point, the inebriate finds himself a "drug addict" without being made aware of his deterioration in the same sense that he would have been if he had taken morphine.

Because of this similarity between the more commonly accepted neuroses and alcoholism, much of the treatment that has been found beneficial in the former is applicable to the latter. Even before the advent of psychoanalysis, one of the cardinal methods of approach to functional disorders of the mind has been through an analysis of the patient's past and present life to the end that the afflicted may unburden themselves, and that as much light as possible may be shed on the underlying motivations through expression. Furthermore, an intimate discussion with a sympathetic listener whose opinion is believed to be authoritative generally brings distinct relief to a troubled mind, even though no advice is given. Frequently I have been thanked at the close of an interview for the assistance I have rendered, when that assistance has consisted merely in being an interested audience. Unconsciously the patient has drawn off his emotional pressure, the driving force behind his undesired state of mind and the conduct resulting from it. If there is live steam in the boiler, it must either go into the cylinder or escape through the safety valve. If the engine cannot revolve and the safety valve is jammed, the boiler bursts. This is an apt if somewhat crude simile of what happens to the neurotic, though the bursting may be expressed in symptoms ranging from a fear of subways to chronic drunkenness.

2. Occupation

While the past is doubtless responsible in one way or another for present conditions, the future is going to determine whether or not these conditions are to be changed. To be more explicit, the pursuit of suitable work and the enjoyment of interesting hobbies are without doubt the easiest and surest method of substituting sensible ideas for stupid ones. The discovery of an interesting occupation to which the nervous system is suited is certainly one of the most important goals to be striven for in the reeducation of alcoholics. If a suitable occupation can be selected in advance, much effort, often useless, in trying to adapt a personality to an unsuitable one can be avoided. A man with an unstable nervous system cannot successfully carry on a business which perpetually worries him even though it may be interesting.

As an incitement to seek the relief of alcohol, invariably go worry, boredom, and discouragement. An occupation may be in itself distasteful; lack of future opportunity may produce a sense of futility. The energy, both physical and psychic, that a person can expend beneficially depends much less on the quantity of the work than on the quality of the emotional reaction to it. Where a person is continually performing a disagreeable task, he is in a constant state of conflict, though he may be unaware of it because of repression. The greater the conflict and the longer its duration, the more the individual feels himself to be trapped. If he reasons, as he generally does, that his condition is no fault of his own stupidity, then he is sure to feel that he is entitled to forget his troubles in intoxication. To combat alcoholism without making every effort to combat what may well be one of the chief external causes is putting undue emphasis on psychological persuasion, which may naturally be unable to carry the whole load in the face of too great an obstacle.

If possible, a man should leave a distasteful job for one which holds out a natural appeal even if the transfer involves a temporary reduction of financial return. This is much easier to write about than to put into effect, but, in general, plans can at least be made for an eventual change so that the individual substitutes for the trapped feeling a more philosophical acceptance of a status which he has come to regard as temporary. Where a change seems to be impossible, depression can often be alleviated by the development of some hobby to be pursued in the evenings and over the week-end. If a man has something to look forward to at the end of the day, time passes more quickly and with considerably less bitterness. Dr. Myerson comes to my support here. "A hobby, or secondary object of interest," he writes, "is therefore a real necessity to a man or woman battling for a purpose whose interest must be sustained. It acts to relax, to shift the excitement, and to allow something of the feeling of novelty as one reapproaches the task."

Where the predominating conscious conflict in a man's life revolves around another personality rather than around a material object, a radical change in the relationship should be deferred if possible until the drink problem has been settled, when a man will act according to the ideas resulting from a free functioning intelligence rather thin those of an unstable alcoholic emotionalism. It is true that he may consider with justification that the other personality, when most displeasing, is a distinct stimulus to his habit. Nevertheless he cannot be sure of his opinions until he finds out by actual trial to what extent both the conduct of this person and his own ideation are a result of chronic drunkenness, occasionally interspersed with grouchy and uncertain periods on the water wagon. (One of my patients who recovered eventually from alcoholism bitterly regretted a divorce which he had prematurely precipitated because of a disorganized state of mind.) An inebriate does not know his own true self. In fact, it is no exaggeration to say that this knowledge does not come in its entirety for many months after a man has been sober on a "for-all-time" basis. The chances are that his drinking started in late adolescence, and thus he has never known either the extent or the direction of his adult potentialities. Therefore all important decisions, other than that definitely to stop drinking, should be postponed until the treatment is well on its way to a successful culmination.

3. The Body

Although this book does not discuss the physiological results of excessive drinking, the attention given the body during the period of mental reeducation requires brief consideration.

In order successfully to make over certain processes of the mind, the organic system should give all the assistance that it can. It should be kept in the best possible condition, and to that end the elements of a normal physical hygiene should be faithfully followed. A medical examination by a competent physician is a wise point of departure to find out what corrections, if any, are necessary to enable the patient to carry on his work with a feeling of physical well-being. A moderate amount of daily exercise— walking is as good as any other —is a requisite for the average person's health. (Anything more strenuous should follow the doctor's advice.) A person who is taking up the reorganization of his mind should employ every means possible to assist him, and quite naturally the condition and training of the body are not the least important.

Because of its extreme obviousness, this essential phase of the work is given only the briefest mention, but that does not mean that it can be slighted—indeed, it must receive the most careful consideration.

4. Relaxation And Suggestion

The next phase of the work is that of relaxation and suggestion. This well-known method of psychotherapy has a twofold purpose. First, to remove the emotional tenseness from the conscious mind; second, to educate the unconscious so that it will function in harmony with the desires of the conscious.

Relaxation, or the elimination of tenseness, comes first. If people accustomed to the use of alcohol will reflect, they will probably agree that the pleasurable state of mind resulting from the first few drinks is due primarily to two mental states—a feeling of self-importance, and an accompanying feeling of calmness, poise, or relaxation. We have already indicated that "self-importance" can be created legitimately and maintained permanently without recourse to alcohol. Relaxation can as easily be achieved by natural methods, and experience has shown over and over again that when this has been the case, a most important blow has been struck at the fundamental causes of excessive drinking. This tension, which is largely emotional, can express itself in a variety of ways; fear, worry, and, most commonly, boredom. Unhappily, for many men, alcohol for a short space of time removes tension most effectively, and so the person disposed to these states of mind has a tendency to resort to it as a narcotic (a quieting drug having strong habit-forming propensities). That alcohol is no real solution to nervous tension is shown when drinking is carried to its extreme limit (delirium tremens). But, whatever the final results may be, the initial effects are so satisfactory that the individual is tempted to seek this method over and over again for want of a better one, with full realization of the eventual suffering that he must endure. On the other hand, if he can find a method which will prevent the accumulation of this excess tension, if he can learn to face life calmly and quietly, he will not feel the need of what he thinks of as a stimulant but what in reality is a sedative. Men, if necessary, can resist a stimulant; but once they employ alcohol as a narcotic they have great difficulty in controlling themselves. When the narcotic employed is very powerful, as is the case with morphine and cocaine, the problem is practically insoluble outside of the four walls of an institution.

Relaxation, however, can be achieved without alcohol if a person will take the time to study the method. Let us consider for a moment the physical aspect. When a man can go through the day using only those muscles which he needs at the time and to the extent that the situation demands and can permit them to recuperate the rest of the time through relaxation, he is far more efficient in business and far less fatigued when the day's work is over than he is if, for example, he sits at his desk with his legs rigid and his toes dug into his shoes or walks home at the end of the day with his Jaws and fists clenched. From the mental point of view, if this same man can train himself by methods of relaxation to avoid displays of temper, baseless apprehensions, shyness, and other unpleasant moods, not by attempting to suppress them, but by finding out why they exist and anticipating occasions which might create them, he has begun to get at the roots of his drinking in a manner that he never did when he was putting the blame on his inheritance, the bad start he got in college—or the weather.

Now let us consider the phenomena of suggestion.

The existence of the unconscious (sub-conscious or co-conscious) and the fact that it can be affected, without even the knowledge of the conscious, were definitely proved long ago by hypnotism. Thus if all in need of it could be hypnotized, and if the effects of hypnotism were permanent, the whole problem of alcoholism would be solved by this method of treatment. Unfortunately, however, many persons cannot be hypnotized (this is particularly true of introverts, who make up the largest group of alcoholics), and those who can are in most cases only temporarily relieved of their ailments. In fact, it was because of the limitations of hypnotism that Freud was impelled to seek other methods to treat successfully the psychoneuroses, and thus finally evolved psychoanalysis. He was perfectly capable of putting many of his patients in a state of hypnosis, and of giving them, while in that state, suggestions that were of the utmost benefit for the time being, but because of the ultimate recurrence of the malady he was dissatisfied with it as a means of psychotherapy. On the other hand, it has been found by many practitioners that a deep though fully conscious relaxation (what the late Dr. Morton Prince called a state of abstraction) followed by suggestion seems to give the unconscious mind the stimulation and direction that it needs. As the patient is well aware of what is taking place, the results of this suggestion are not as quick and spectacular as they are when amnesia is induced, but they are surer and in the long run their effect is out of all proportion to the energy spent in practicing them, provided the work is carried on systematically over a sufficient period of time. Let him who is skeptical about this suggestion commit to memory two verses of poetry-one in the morning to recite in the evening, and the other just before going to sleep to recite on the following morning. He will soon discover that the latter gives better results with a minimum of effort expended.

The relaxation procedure is as follows. The patient is instructed to recline in a chair and think of himself as being numb, heavy, limp, and relaxed. He is told that the chair and the floor are holding him up and that there is no need for him to make any effort whatsoever. He need not even keep perfectly quiet if it is difficult for him to do so. If other ideas than those he is being given enter his mind, he is warned not to try to resist them but to let them come into his field of thought and then quietly pass out of it again. He takes a long deep breath in the beginning which is slowly exhaled, and thereafter the breathing is rhythmical and slow as in sleep. In a voice that is even and monotonous the instructor enumerates the more prominent muscles of the body, such as the arms, legs, shoulders, and back, which are to be relaxed, and the patient is informed many times that he is becoming drowsier and sleepier, and that his mind is following his body into a state of relaxation. When at the end of four or five minutes a state of drowsiness has been attained, simple suggestions are given; but these suggestions must under no circumstances conflict with ideas which are acceptable to the individual when he is in alert condition.

He is then instructed to relax himself at night in much the same manner, though he is at perfect liberty to invent any method of his own which he may find more effective in treating himself. For instance, one patient discovered that relaxation could best be induced under conditions of extreme tension by first making the muscles all over the body as taut as possible while slowly inhaling, and then very slowly relaxing while exhaling, the process to be repeated more and more slowly as often as necessary.

The suggestions given to the patient during the relaxed state are in general to the effect that he is going to be more calm, poised, and relaxed on the following day, that he is slowly but surely building up a well-poised mature personality, and that as his nervous tension passes away the desire for alcohol will go with it; furthermore, that through a relaxed attitude he will develop a sense of relativity so that he can distinguish the true values of life from the false, and that, what is all-important, having distinguished them, he will be able to develop them in a sustained manner.

Alcohol itself is referred to as briefly as possible because of the danger of employing negatively suggestive words, but in the beginning it is necessary to mention it if the subject is to be done sufficient justice in the patient's estimation.

If, on retiring, a person is already relaxed and ready for sleep; the artificial method can be dispensed with, but the suggestion must never be omitted as the ideas in the mind at that particular moment are more potent in influencing the personality than at any other time.

A whole book might be—and indeed has been—written on the energy wasted and the exhaustion produced by living in a contracted state of mind and body. Bodily tension, except where it is willed for the accomplishment of some task, is always the result of a nervous state of mind, though the latter can exist apparently independent of physical expression. For those who are interested in the physiological side of this problem I recommend Progressive Relaxation, by Dr. Edmund Jacobson. It is rather technical for a layman, but it shows in a convincing manner the far-reaching results of relaxation.

I appreciate that this relaxation-suggestion phase of the treatment may sound like hocus-pocus to those who have never tried it. But I have never yet seen a person––and alcoholics are much more apt to be skeptical than credulous––who did not admit receiving very distinct benefits from it, once they had given it a fair trial.

It must be clearly understood, however, that relaxation is the direct opposite rather than the counterpart of laziness and slouchiness. (The sporting columns of Mr. Grantland Rice have made much of relaxation as an all-important element in a successful athletic career.) Relaxation is, in fact, the antithesis of laziness, in that by conservation of energy greater efficiency is promoted, and hence more successful work can be accomplished. Catching a baseball is a good simile to illustrate the difference between the tense and relaxed attitude towards life. A novice holds out his hands rigidly; the ball strikes them, stings, and is probably muffed. A trained player extends his hands to meet the ball, but brings them back at the moment of contact; there is no pain, and the ball has been caught, because relaxation has taken place at the proper moment.

To substantiate the theory I have described, quotations from Mr. Courtenay Baylor's book, Remaking a Man, are pertinent. "I recognized," he writes, "that the taking of the tabooed drink was the physical expression of a certain temporary but recurrent mental condition which appeared to be a combination of wrong impulses and a wholly false, though plausible philosophy. Further, I believed that these strange periods were due to a condition of the brain which seemed akin to a physical tension and which set up in the processes a peculiar shifting and distorting and imagining of values; and I have found that with a release of this 'tenseness' a normal coordination does come about, bringing proper impulses and rational thinking."

And again, "Underlying and apparently causing this mental state (fear, depression, or irritability), I have always found the brain condition which suggests actual physical tenseness. In this condition a brain never senses things as they really are. As the tenseness develops, new and imaginary values arise and existing values change their relative positions of importance and become illogical and irrational. Ideas at other times unnoticed or even scorned become, under tenseness, so insistent that they are converted into controlling impulses. False values and false thinking run side by side with the normal philosophy for a time; and then with the increasing tenseness the abnormal attitude gradually replaces the normal in control. This is true whether the particular question be one of drinking or of giving way to some other impulse; the same indecision, changeability, inconsistency, and lack of resistance mark the mental process. In fact, the person will behave like one or the other of two different individuals as he or she is not mentally tense."

We must not overlook one very important but little-recognized stimulus to drinking. Emotional instability (tension) can be created by legitimate excitement (such as attending a football game where the home team is victorious or, for that matter, by any other form of pleasant emotional stimulation) just as surely as it can by worry and unhappiness. In fact, it would be no exaggeration to say that the alcoholic has to learn to withstand success just as assuredly as he does misfortune, strange as this statement may seem. Many drunkards claim that they do not use alcohol as a refuge but as a means of celebration, and they are probably right as far as their conscious minds are concerned.

Why a man under pleasant emotional stimulation seeks narcotic escape from reality in the same manner as he does from unpleasant emotions is an interesting question but difficult to answer. My own theory is that a neurotic is unconsciously, and possibly consciously, afraid when his emotional equilibrium is disturbed, no matter what the quality of the disturbance may be. When he is in a state of euphoria (happiness) he evidently feels the need of a stabilizer to the same extent as he does in dysphoria (unhappiness). Just as he is bored when he looks inward, so he is frightened when he looks outward, if the customary scene has changed even a little.

Stekel, the psychoanalyst, throws some light on this question when he writes in his volume, The Beloved Ego: "There has always remained a bitter sediment in every joy, a secret fear that 'the gods wish to destroy us,' that happiness would be followed by misfortune, and that the contrast would make the inevitable misfortune appear all the greater. Is this the right form of teaching? Happiness should not make us reckless; but should our happiness be poisoned by the thought of its inevitable end?"

Is it not possible that this "bitter sediment" is overdeveloped in the alcoholic, even if it is entirely unconscious?

Finally, we must remember that most people enjoy being emotional, and would like to express themselves in this instinctive manner much more often than is possible under normal living conditions, and the resistance to such expression for lack of opportunity is a contributing cause of tension. When men drink, the self-critical inhibitions are lowered and an emotional discharge easily takes place.

"Now of all the intellectual functions," says Professor McDougall, "that of self-criticism is the highest and latest developed, for in it are combined the functions of critical judgment and of self-consciousness, that self-knowledge which is essential to the supreme activity we call volition or the deliberative will. It is the blunting of this critical side of self-awareness by alcohol, and the consequent setting free of the emotions and their instinctive impulses from its habitual control, that give to the convivial drinker the aspect and the reality of a general excitement."

The individual under the influence of alcohol does what he wants to do,—that is, in some way exercises his emotions,—and he is happy doing anything so long as he can have this emotional outlet. It matters very little from the point of view of a good time whether he laughs or cries, and, for that matter, whether he cries over the death of a friend or the blowing out of an automobile tire. If tears and sobs are any indication of his grief, they both furnish the same amount of sorrow. In other words, alcohol not only permits an emotional discharge, but also it never fails to provide an instantaneous incitement to whatever new emotional form of expression comes to mind. However ridiculous this incitement and its form of expression may be from the sober point of view, they are satisfying to the drinker. He has his "cause" and he is going to have his emotional spree about it. (The word "emotion" is used in a wide sense in this particular paragraph. For instance, to be very serious-minded and persuasive about nothing at all would certainly be an emotional rather than an intellectual proceeding.)

While the release of the emotions through alcohol may be of benefit to the normal drinker who has an occasional "party," it in no sense releases the alcoholic, but on the contrary precipitates him into a worse mental condition than he was in at the beginning. The moment he regains sobriety a new series of depressive nervous thoughts are in attendance to take the place of the boredom or worry that was supposed to have been the cause of the first drink.

So the alcoholic must learn, not to eliminate or repress, but through relaxation to prevent the accumulation of emotional tension unaided by alcohol. There are certainly times when the emotions should be enjoyed to the limit, and the person who is always restrained and judicial is apt to be a dull pedant. But once a legitimate emotional situation is over, a man must learn to revert willingly to the realm of reason until another normal moment for emotionalism presents itself. These occasions should not be prolonged or created on a whim by indulging in a drug which is too stimulating in the beginning and far too depressing for a long time thereafter. The results in the long run are as futile as they are when this same substance is used as a refuge from trouble.

As a matter of fact, one of the most interesting features to observe about drink, and the one that more than any other has made it an alluring social custom, is its apparent soothing and yet stimulating effects acting simultaneously. These attributes seem to have a fatal fascination for those whose nervous systems are not suited to being stimulated or relaxed by an artificial medium. Coffee will stimulate and sleeping powders soothe, but neither of them creates a feeling of elation, whereas alcohol in its earliest stages seems to possess both the "desired" qualifications. Of course these effects are only temporary. It is common knowledge that the stimulation resulting from liquor is so short-lived and so quickly turns to exhaustion that nobody contemplating prolonged effort considers employing it as an aid. Even more deceptive is the soothing quality, for, as has been stated, the continued drinking of unlimited quantities of alcohol results in delirium tremens, the very peak of physical and mental tension.

5. Reading And Writing

It is often helpful in influencing the trend of thinking to read books of a constructive nature whether they bear directly on the problem, as would be the case with those of a philosophical or psychological nature, or whether the appeal is through inference. Books which would influence in this manner are biographies or autobiographies of men who have become successful.

Lives of such men as Napoleon, Lincoln, Lee, Washington, Pasteur, and Disraeli cannot fail to act as an inspiration to a man who is endeavoring to get rid of an undesirable habit. Conversely, literature which deals with the charms of hedonism, which expounds a philosophy of "Eat, drink, and be merry, for to-morrow we die," or which glowingly describes dissipation, should be carefully avoided until the patient is definitely cured.

Of those books which deal directly with the problem of character integration in a popular manner I know of none better than The Human Machine, by Arnold Bennett. There are, of course, others written in a similar vein, and if the alcoholic will give a little attention to the bookstores and libraries he will be able to find sufficient reading material to keep his mind constructively occupied throughout the period of treatment.

How much, if any, investigation of abnormal psychology should be made depends upon the individual reaction to the subject. For instance, some men are quite interested in the theories of psychoanalysis and can read its more simplified expositions with considerable benefit, while others are disturbed by it, or merely disinterested.

Such books as interest the patient must be read in a careful manner, and the ideas which particularly appeal to him should be marked. This does not mean that an abstract is to be made as proof that the book has been read with understanding, but rather that the patient is to gather together a group of ideas which will contribute to the construction of a new philosophy of life. If a few helpful suggestions can be culled from pages of platitudes, then reading the book has been worthwhile. For this reason a person should show some degree of perseverance in searching through a book which may not stimulate him in the beginning. On the other hand, if he has a definitely unpleasant reaction to it, he should drop it instantly.

Writing as well as reading is of benefit to the patient. It helps to crystallize in his mind the ideas that he has received. He may write an exposition of his personal reaction to the treatment so far as he has progressed in it, or he may write a letter to an imaginary friend describing how the alcoholic habit can be eliminated. If this latter way is employed, the patient is for the moment playing the role of teacher, and there is no way of learning that is half as effective as teaching.

Writing incidentally will disclose how many of the ideas have been thoroughly understood and retained in the patient's mind, how many have gone in one ear and out the other, and how many have been twisted so that they are more in line with emotional wish fulfillment than with an intellectual disposition of the problem under consideration. Many people who are apparently listening with the closest attention are in reality only considering what they themselves are going to say when it comes their turn to do the talking. Whatever the method of approach to the composition, the cure will be clarified, objectified, and in a sense intensified by an occasional thesis of not less than two pages. If an individual is willing to write more often and at length, so much the better.

The following is a sample theme of the autobiographical type, written by a man for whom alcohol had become a serious problem because of his occasional antisocial reaction to a normal amount, rather than because of prolonged debauches. He felt with some reason that this latter manifestation was latent.

The cure for alcoholism, as given me during the last nine months, has left me with the following impressions.

When I began the cure, I had just reached the

point when alcohol had become a narcotic. The periods during which I was "on the wagon" were becoming shorter and shorter, and in the ensuing "hangovers" I had already reached the point when I felt that I needed rather than wanted a drink the next day. My shame and depression from the periodic outbreaks was becoming a dull and ever present misery.

I had for some time known that Peabody was making a business of successfully curing alcoholics, and after an especially severe debauch I called him in on the theory that it was at least worthwhile for me to hear about how other people had been cured. The first, and one of the most important, things that I got out of his explanation was a brand new thought to me— namely, that habit of thought is more powerful than will. This thought immediately reduced the cure from an intangible exercise of will power to a definite course of mental training, and made the cure seem to me not conceivable but probable. It made the cure seem more like learning algebra than learning to love Art.

Starting from the basic idea that, although it involved a great deal of effort, it was possible, I then considered the question of whether it was worthwhile to make the effort. The answer was obvious.

The answer to the next necessary decision to be

made by me was equally obvious. If I was to change my habit of thought, learn to want not to drink, I must give up alcohol for all time, as only by doing so could I eliminate any conflict of thought on the subject.

From this point on the cure became an exercise of mental gymnastics, the overrunning of old habits of thought by new habits of thought. You cannot obliterate tracks in the mind any more than you can hoof prints in a muddy road, but you can overrun those old tricks in the mind until they are no longer important in the same way that you can overrun hoof prints in a muddy road by the tire tracks of an automobile.

One of the tasks I was set seems very important to me—the making out of a daily schedule, which, once made out, had to be lived up to. This issuance of small commands to myself and my obedience to them rapidly restored my self-respect. Incidentally my efficiency in my daily work was enormously increased, which increased the respect for me of other people. This reacted favorably on my confidence in myself. In other words, by perfectly mechanical means I was enabled to run what had been a vicious circle into a beneficent circle. The more pride I was able to take in myself the less need I had of the rallying effect of alcohol when I went out.

Besides the schedule, another aid was available and equally important. Almost all impulses originate in the unconscious mind. It is necessary therefore to change the habit of thought in the unconscious mind. This is perfectly possible. Peabody used to—and still does—relax me, physically as well as mentally, and when I am in a relaxed condition, talks to me. What thoughts he expresses at that time are sowed in my unconscious mind. He has taught me to do the same thing for myself. The result is that when I am offered a cocktail, instead of instinctively saying "Yes" I instinctively say "No." I have been able to put the application of this method to work in my daily life downtown.

All this sounds pretty easy. It is not easy for several reasons. First, that it takes a certain amount of courage to admit that you, yourself, cannot do what others can apparently successfully do, namely, drink. Secondly, that it takes a long time to overrun with new habits of thought the old habits of thought in the mind, and a certain amount of will power is necessary to carry you through the long grind.

After my common sense told me that the cure was possible,—in fact, if the work be done, inevitable,—I went to Peabody on the same theory that I would have gone to in instructor of mathematics had I found it necessary to learn calculus. Probably

I could learn calculus by myself out of books, but it would take me a great deal longer than if I went to a competent teacher. I keep referring to mathematics because the whole cure seems to me similar to addition. If you add two and two you get four. If you add one and two you don't get four, you only get three. What you put into your mind you take out. If, over a long period of time, you have put things into your mind which are bad for you those same things come out, and the reason that I am so much better off to-day than I was nine months ago is that the right things that I have been putting into my mind have largely nullified the wrong things that I had put in the past.

6. Living By Schedule

The therapeutic problem is one of mental and emotional reintegration, which implies obviously that a disintegration of personality is found to some extent in each patient at the beginning of the work. This disintegration shows itself in laziness and inefficiency; even when the alcoholic is sober. This it is absolutely necessary to correct. Of course there are some inebriates who from time to time introduce bursts of efficiency into an otherwise disordered life. Then there are those who concentrate upon one form of "efficiency" so that it is almost a fetish. Neatness is a case in point. I have known drunkards who prided themselves upon their personal appearance at all times (except when they were so drunk that they did not know what they were doing), even though their life was crumbling about their ears. But by and large the excessive drinker has lost his sense of values; he has no goal in life; he is entirely concerned with drinking, sobering up, and drinking again. Everything else is of so little importance that it receives at best only a halfhearted consideration, and, more often, none at all. The "conscientious" acts performed when under the influence of liquor would have been better left undone until sobriety was again attained.

The individual who leads this sort of inefficient existence, even when he is not an alcoholic, is flying in the face of an urge having almost instinctive force, for whenever we observe nature we note an orderly system. This same methodical urge to be integrated exists in our characters. In olden times this question of conduct was such an obsession that the word "integrity" itself, which originally meant orderliness, came to assume a definitely ethical meaning. Nowadays to be well organized is recognized as a concrete means of existence rather than an abstract principle with religious overtones. Dr. Jelliffe and Dr. White, in the chapter on the Manic-Depressive psychoses in their book, Diseases of the Nervous System say, "The efficiency of one's relation to reality is the measure of one's normality."

Our problem is to substitute a benign for a vicious circle, and the key to this substitution is the employment of a method whereby a relative degree of efficiency will be achieved. The drunkard must naturally sober up first; but, this having been accomplished; a new and more vigorous point of view must be injected into that period which heretofore has consisted in marking time between "parties," to take the place of indifference, remorse, or hopeless discouragement. If, during this interim, the reaction to life can be changed even slightly for the better, if some concrete action can be introduced into the daily attempt at normal adaptation which will give the patient the feeling, "Here is something constructive (dynamic and new)," then the cure may be said to have started.

I say "concrete" action because wise planning is a comparatively easy task for most people. In fact, it is so easy that all but the most vicious inebriates have been as full of lofty and sensible ideas as they have been of liquor, long before they have taken any constructive action about their problem. But it is the execution of the plan that determines whether or not the initial theories were of any value. There must be action—forceful, purposive, intelligent, and sustained; and there is no better way to produce this action than to plan and execute one's life according to a self-imposed, prearranged schedule. To be explicit: before going to bed the patient should write down on a piece of paper the different hours of the following day, beginning with the time of arising. Then, so far as can be determined beforehand, he should fill in these hours with what he plans to do. Throughout the day notations should be made if exceptions have occurred in the original plans, and it should be indicated whether these exceptions have been due to legitimate or rationalized excuses. The latter must be avoided at all costs. Small as well as large activities that are taken up should not be dropped until completed unless they are in a sense unknown quantities, entered upon for purposes of investigation only.

Just how detailed the schedule should be depends somewhat upon the individual personality, for it is the spirit in which it is carried out rather than the letter of the law that is important. Some people are made nervous by looking at the clock, and so they have better results if they merely put down what they intend to do in a semblance of order. The time method is the best, however, although it is desirable that the commitments should not be treated from a petty point of view, such as might create only an annoying reaction. For instance, when a person his set aside the hours from three to five for reading, he is not supposed to close his book promptly at five o'clock if a few minutes more will give him sufficient time to finish the chapter. Moreover, there are business as well as social interests which cannot be terminated at any hour known in advance, as they depend upon other people who are not in any way interested in a schedule. Obviously, under these conditions, question marks will have to be substituted for definite time limits, but this need not prevent the schedule from doing all that it is intended to do if such things as can be done are carried out in the proper spirit.

The schedule must be thorough; on it goes everything—not only work and duty, but pleasure and rest, though the rest should be of a definite nature and not just loafing about. At least one thing which must be done eventually, but which has been procrastinated because it is distasteful, should be included in each day's plan until all the pieces of an inefficient past have been picked up.

As far as notations go, I wish to repeat for emphasis that these will be determined by common sense, checked by the utmost personal honesty that can possibly be attained. Most people in their hearts cannot really fool themselves unless they wish to. So the alcoholic should have no trouble in determining honestly whether a change in the schedule has been made for sensible and necessary reasons or whether it has come about through the reassertion of the old habits of laziness, if logical, it should be made without hesitation, for the schedule has reason as its basis and not fanaticism; but ingenious as well as feeble excuses must be stringently suppressed.

The schedule contributes to the reintegration of character in three ways, all of them important. First, it prevents idleness. This advantage is so obvious that I shall let a quotation from Dr. Stekel suffice for further comment. "Earthly happiness," he writes, "or that condition which we call happiness, is primarily dependent upon our relationship to time. People who have no time, but, in spite of that, find time for everything they wish to do, are the happiest. There is no need for them to kill time. They never get so far as to become conscious of it—they know no boredom. Boredom is nothing else than consciousness of time."

Second, the schedule brings to the attention of the alcoholic the fact that he is doing something concrete about changing his condition, something more than mere discussion and reflection. One of the chief difficulties of the treatment is its seeming vagueness outside of the central theme (abstinence), and so the more reality that can be brought into the work, the surer and quicker the favorable outcome.

As has been stated before, the alcoholic is more of a student than a patient, and he should never be allowed to forget that he is taking a course.

The third and most important of all reasons for employing the schedule is the training that it gives the individual in executing his own commands. It stands to reason that if ten or twenty times each day a person carries out a self-imposed direction, even though each of these directions may in itself be infinitesimal, a definite contribution has been made to the formation of a new character.

In battle it has been proved over and over again that large hordes of individually brave but untrained men can accomplish little when opposed by a smaller but disciplined military group. It takes plenty of close order drill before a regiment can go over the top, though the commands of that drill are never by any chance used in modern warfare.

So with the alcoholic and his temptation. He cannot expect consistently to conquer his enemy in every drawing-room and country-club porch if he has made no advance preparation. He must do something more than theorize, important as that is, if he is going to pass through a cocktail barrage unscathed. In the end, to be sure, his abstinence will be the result of his not actually wanting to drink, but to reach that end successfully requires a disciplined personality. That this training, if carried out over a sufficient period of time, will have ultimate results far exceeding that of mere sobriety goes without saying, but we will reserve discussion of that important "by-product" for a later period.

From my own point of view the schedule gives a very good indication of what may be expected from each particular patient. A man who cannot or will not carry out such an important element of the work may be strongly suspected of being unsuitable material upon which to spend time and energy either because of his constitutional makeup or because of lack of sincerity.

7. The Notebook And Will Power

Keeping a notebook is another helpful means of objectifying the work. As a basis for this book I have collected some sixty statements pertaining to the elimination of the alcoholic habit. These ideas, which average about one hundred and fifty words each, are set down on separate sheets of paper, one of which the patient takes home with him, after it has been carefully discussed, and transcribes in his own handwriting. He is cautioned to do this work only when he has sufficient time to give the point under consideration considerable reflection. If he can expand the idea, or if he can express it, without changing the sense, in words that make more of an appeal to him, so much the better.

He also copies into his notebook those ideas which he has marked in the books that he has read. Thus he creates a personal reference book which should stimulate him by precept, warning, or inference toward better control and more mature behavior. This book he should turn to frequently for the purpose of refreshing his mind with his new system of philosophy and as a means of correcting any negative suggestion which he may have absorbed.

Of course it is the spirit with which the notebook is kept that is important, not the perfunctory copying out of so many words in an uncritical and unreflective frame of mind. If the alcoholic cannot see the help to be derived from this procedure, as in the case of the schedule, he should not be coerced into taking it up. But the conscientious student who wishes to make the most of his time will be anxious to employ all the elements that have assisted others toward reconstruction. There are too few of these aids as it is, and it is hardly fair if one or two are neglected, particularly as the one that is slighted is presumably the one that is most necessary. "Many patients," writes Dr. Menninger, "show their resistance by doing everything imaginable in the name of treatment, except the thing most likely to cure them."

For example, if exercise is avoided, the mind has to work against, rather than with, a body which at least should be pulling its own weight. If, again, the pre-sleep suggestion is forgotten, the unconscious is not being trained to cooperate with the conscious, and thus one of the strongest methods of attacking the problem is omitted.

I have emphasized the right spirit in which the work should be undertaken and maintained. Anticipation is a powerful aid to this proper frame of mind. The alcoholic must continually suggest to himself that he is going to carry on the work just as conscientiously and seriously in the future as he did in the beginning until he has had a year of uninterrupted sobriety behind him. If he faithfully faces the future in this manner, he will be well armed against overconfidence or laziness, (if he is sane and sincere, there is no chance of an "about face" as regards his intellectual attitude.)

In the beginning he is particularly apt to get good results, because, although he is very near to the latest expression of the habit he is endeavoring to conquer, the treatment is colored with novelty and enthusiasm. When this wears off, as it is bound to do, he may become lazy and uninterested if he has not taken pains to prepare his future mental attitude, though the method that this laziness will take will be a premature conviction that he is already cured. Experience has shown that relapses come about in this way and not because of the accumulation of an irresistible thirst through a period of abstinence. As a matter of fact, in no case yet where a relapse has occurred has the patient told me that it resulted from overwhelming temptation in spite of conscientious work. In each and every instance it was frankly admitted that the carrying out of the therapeutic measures had been allowed to slacken some time before a drink was actually taken. There have been a few instances which might be considered an exception to this statement in its narrowest sense. These occurred very early in the treatment and were the sudden expression of rage or grief which gave the neophyte the "justification" he was looking for.

Before finishing the discussion of the treatment, there is one point which I should like to bring home. So much has been said about methods for overcoming the alcoholic habit other than the old-fashioned one of straight will power that the reader may be wondering if this does not enter into the work at all. On this point there should be no misunderstanding. Will power is most decidedly necessary, but after the first month or two it is used chiefly as a force to compel the patient to carry on his work. It is much more effective if applied in this manner than if it is blindly directed against the habit itself. The latter method might be described as will power fighting with its bare fists, and the former as will power armed with an assortment of weapons with which to coerce an errant mind. If the will is used without any imagination in a headlong and unscientific attack, if all effort is concentrated on the control of the habit and none on the redirecting of the desires, sooner or later will power will lose and a long (?) period on the wagon will be the best that can be said for the energy expended.

But while the new habits are forming, the will must be used without stint whenever necessary. The treatment is founded on common sense and sound psychological principles rather than magic, and there is no known means for removing instantaneously the desire for alcohol forever. At later periods also there may be times when, in spite of all his efforts, the patient frankly wants to drink. But he will be tempted less intensely as time passes and far less frequently, so that it can do him no harm to fall back on will power to tide him over his occasional "crises," conscious that his temptation will be short-lived and in the end entirely eliminated.

The question of will power has been stressed because one or two individuals have conceived the idea, probably as a result of wish-fulfillment, that the treatment would instantly remove the desire for drink and that will power did not enter into the matter; that therefore if they really wanted to drink they might do so, leaving the future change in point of view to some transcendental power. They were right about will power not entering into the matter after the cure has been completed, but to try this theory at the beginning of the treatment when they were naturally full of thirsty associations was the worst form of sophistry and rationalization.

8. Pitfalls

It is, I believe, desirable to warn the alcoholic of certain pitfalls. While we cannot say that such a caution is synonymous with prevention, nevertheless knowledge of motives and reactions is certainly of great help in the science of controlling the emotions. These ideas, which might be called a mental defensive preparation, are not necessarily linked together except as they apply to the central theme, nor are they set forth in order of importance.

It would hardly seem necessary to devote space to the discussion of "systematic drinking" at this late period in the book if an attempt to utilize the treatment as a means of drinking moderately had not actually been put in practice by an unusually intelligent and sincere patient. At the time, to be sure, his reasoning was unconscious, and so there was no reversal of policy toward drinking as an accepted way of life, but when the smoke of a temporary explosion had cleared away, it would seem that the philosophy evolved was as follows: "I have learned how to stop drinking and am happy without it. Two or three times a year, however, I should like to drink moderately during the evening. I am so satisfied without liquor and have such a good system for directing and controlling emotional thinking that I am sure I shall be able to restrict my indulgence to the amount stated."

This was a beautiful theory, and those who are not aware of the insidious power that alcohol has over certain organisms might be disposed to find it logical. The trouble with this "reasoning" was that the results were very different from those intended, for the patient frankly and voluntarily admitted that after a six months' trial it was a complete failure and that his drinking was more of a fiasco than it had ever been before.

The alcoholic cannot make plans and set limitations for the use of alcohol, for once he has taken a drink he ceases to be himself in a much deeper meaning of the phrase than would be applicable to the average man under the influence of liquor. To be sure, this does not always show at the beginning of a "party." In fact, it is perfectly possible that on occasions the alcoholic may take his normal drinking friend home and put him to bed. But the behavior on succeeding days proves the truth of the statement that alcohol for inebriates acts as a mental-nerve poison in a manner that it does not for the normal drinker, regardless of the comparative condition of the two in the early stages of what is to be an evening's dissipation for one and a debauch for the other.

As has been mentioned before, alcoholism is a disease of immaturity, regardless of the actual age of the individual suffering from it. The drunkard is not only a child, but a spoiled child. He has far too keen a sensibility for likes and dislikes, chiefly the latter. By trying to avoid everything unpleasant and make what he cannot avoid artificially enjoyable, he reaches a state wherein he likes nothing when sober. He must be reeducated in a manner that will show him that, while a diversity of interests is desirable, it is not necessary to like everything, nor is it possible to escape entirely from unpleasant duties. Many of these tasks could perfectly well be done automatically—that is, without endowing them with any emotional consideration whatsoever. They are not important enough to either like or dislike.

As far as the pleasures go, if an ex-alcoholic finds under a sober regime that he dislikes certain things that he enjoyed while drinking, he need not be surprised, but may feel certain that these same things have no genuine interest for him or it would not be necessary for him to whip up an agreeable reaction to them with alcohol. For instance, if, at the age of thirty-five or forty, he finds that he does not like dances when sober, all well and good. Dances are not a criterion of intelligence or necessary as a diversion, and he does not have to attend them. If he objects that staying at home leaves him "out of things," reflection, when he regains his sense of relativity, should show him that he is not "out" of very much, and that a mind functioning soberly over a sufficient period will unquestionably provide a substitute which will make life more interesting and vital for him than formal social activity. Naturally, the more means people have of amusing themselves, the better—and this most certainly includes a social life! But where pleasure cannot be enjoyed unstimulated, and for its own sake, it may be eliminated without self-pity or disparagement.

It is most important that a person who is conscientiously endeavoring to reorganize his morale should understand that 100 per cent results are not necessarily expected. Lapses are bound to occur, but these are seldom serious if immediately checked. (When I say "lapses," I do not refer to actually taking a drink, but rather to a careless, lazy form of behavior.) The worst that can be said of the great majority of such slips is that they tend to create a precedent for future conduct. A whole day or even a week may be wasted because of such an idea as this: "I have made a bad beginning this morning, so I might just as well wait until tomorrow to turn over a new leaf." We all know people who are always waiting for New Year's Day or the first of the month to make a fresh start. They have good intentions, but they never accomplish their purpose. If a slip is checked instantly, however, and a vigorous attitude intervenes the minute the error is recognized, no harm has been done; if a laissez faire policy is adopted for the rest of the day, actual drunkenness may result before nightfall.

Of course, this theory of the harmlessness of a lapse in conduct must not be used as the basis for deliberately creating mistakes, or a very different light would be shed on the picture. The initial mistake is inconsequential only if it is immediately checked and when it has not been premeditated. For an individual to feel that he could err in small ways whenever he happened to feel like it would be flying in the face of common sense, but such twisted ratiocinations are not uncommon to the most intelligent and sincere.

Victories over temptations lead of course to ultimate success, but they must be watched carefully or they may be turned into temporary defeats of a most unexpected, discouraging, and bewildering nature.

One man, attending a class reunion, apparently enjoyed the first two days completely sober. He was delighted to find that he did not want to drink, and, in fact, was having "a damn good time without it." Toward the end of the third day, he suddenly and for no good reason, as he thought, became hopelessly drunk. Another man went through an entire New Year's celebration without a drop, only to find himself getting drunk alone on the second of January when all his friends had finished their carousing. Both of these men were very much upset and amazed at their behavior, though they had heard of others who had done the same thing.

The causes of this apparent strange reversal of conduct are in reality not so obscure and peculiar as they seem at first glance. In the first place, these individuals, whose new habits were by no means crystallized, were undergoing a great deal of concentrated alcoholic suggestion, and they used little constructive reasoning to counteract its effect. In the second place, they were putting up much more resistance of the tense, repressive type than they had any idea of.

After the victorious fight was over, they completely dropped their guard; but their opponent was still on his feet, and before they knew it they themselves were taking the count. An alcoholic who has won a victory may congratulate himself all he wants to, but let his success make him particularly careful of his subsequent behavior. Liquor is always obtainable, and if a man really wants to drink he does not care a hoot whether it is New Year's or any other day.

Because of the power of suggestion, a person should not expose himself to too strong and lengthy temptations during the first six months or so of his treatment. Some people retire from social activity completely, but this is not recommended unless it is proved necessary since there is a happy medium between complete retreat and overexposure. If the individual in process of ridding himself of drinking attends wet parties, he must give himself plenty of positive suggestion before, during, and afterwards, lest what he has seen, heard, and smelt shall cause him to reverse his conduct when such an "excuse" for drinking as there might have been in the beginning has passed away.

In addition to negative suggestion and fatigue, overconfidence can also enter into the situation in a destructive manner. A cured alcoholic may well take satisfaction in his achievement, but he cannot afford to become "cocky"" about his temperance until it is a settled question of many years' standing. As a matter of fact, at that time he will not bother to become "cocky" about it. When he thinks of his drinking career he will merely wonder how he could have been such a fool, he will be glad that he gave it up before it was too late, and he will expend his pride on those things that he achieved as a result of his sobriety.

It is important to add that these preparations can be carried to such an extreme that the occasion itself receives the concentration of attention rather than the preparation. Imaginary dragons should not be created for the purpose of slaying them, for they may possibly slay their creator. If parties cannot be approached with confidence, with such a statement as "Of course I shall not be such a fool as to drink" being said and meant, then the inebriate must stay away from them until he has trained his mind sufficiently so that he can say it with conviction. When a man feels that he cannot spend a few hours in sobriety with others who are drinking, he has lost all sense of proportion. He may have to attend a large dinner now and then for business reasons. If it proves to be a rather wet occasion, what of it? What are two or three hours out of a lifetime? At worst he will be bored, but that is nothing to unbalance a properly adjusted comprehension of reality. If he drinks he is a fool, but if he remains sober he is neither a hero nor a martyr, but just an ordinary mortal using the most elemental common sense. It is much easier, having recognized thoroughly the situation, to react to it as a fleeting fraction of a lifetime, unimportant so long as it is passed in sobriety, than it is to conceive of it as a battle-ground upon which an exhausting combat is to be waged.

Excessive drinking is so generally thought of in terms of wickedness or weakness that it's most salient characteristic is completely ignored. This is its supreme stupidity. For a man deliberately to seek pleasure by methods which he knows are going to bring only suffering is such a farcical performance that the drinker himself (for drinkers have an unusually good sense of humor) would be the first to hold his sides laughing if he saw a parallel waste of energy on the part of anyone else outside of the field of alcohol. Just as all normal boys are anxious not to be considered incompetent in athletics, so to be thought stupid is the last thing that a full-grown man with any pretense to normality wishes. This is one of the chief contributions to the inferiority complex which is such a marked characteristic of excessive drinkers. In their hearts they cannot hide from themselves their own crass stupidity. Even in prisons drunkards are held in low repute by criminals because they are where they are as a result of an inferior intelligence rather than a distorted moral point of view. The others have at least a certain misguided skill and courage.

9. The General Effect

The alcoholic patient, and the general public as well, should disabuse their minds of any ideas they may have that it is only strong characters who are able to complete the treatment satisfactorily. As a matter of fact, it is only the pathologically weak who fail. Obviously a person should have a normal amount of common sense, an ability to persevere, and enough breadth of mind to admit the truth when his own experience confronts him with it. But for the overcoming of alcoholism these qualities are found to a sufficient degree in the average man if he sincerely wants to exercise them. He is not asked to warp his mind to fit any exotic theories, nor is he compelled to undergo any hardships of a mental or physical nature. He is merely shown how to train his intellectual processes so that they have enough control over his emotions to enable him to lead a mature normal life.

A person does not need a great deal of perspicacity to recognize that the advantages to be derived from a cure pass far beyond a mere cessation of drinking. That is, of course, an absolutely necessary preliminary, but the overcoming of the habit by a system, and the application of that same system to other weaknesses of character as well as to the making of new and better adjustments to life, will in the long run carry the individual to a point of efficiency and contentment of which he had little or no realization in the dark days when he was seeing the world through a whiskey bottle. A number of men have said that the principles of relaxation, when applied to their business, have been worth many thousands of dollars, to say nothing of the benefit to their state of mind and the increase in their physical efficiency and endurance. Just as they have learned to handle liquor in the only manner possible for them (by complete elimination), so they have learned to handle life instead of letting life handle them. Because of their peace of mind, their increased stamina and self-confidence, depression, moodiness, irritability, and anxiety tend to disappear. Even when they are faced with problems which make these unpleasant states a normal reaction, their poise and judgment prevent the complete demoralization and despair which accompanied them only too easily in their drinking days.

To the beginner this may sound like an Utopia impossible of realization, for the past may seem to have set an ineffaceable seal on the future. As is to be expected, excessive indulgence, long pursued in the face of common sense and frequent warning, often brings one or more concrete disasters in its wake—loss of position, the breaking up of the home, and the alienation of many if not all friends. But experience has shown over and over again that few of these losses are irretrievable.

Of course the world at large cannot be blamed for being slow to recognize the reform of the inebriate. He in particular and his kind in general, have fooled the public too often with their short intervals on the wagon, from which it was so easy to fall. When, however, people become convinced—and they only become so through the observation of concrete results that the individual really means business, the past is definitely forgotten and forgiven. In fact, the ex-alcoholic will at times be embarrassed at the lavishness of the praise he receives for merely adjusting himself to life in an obviously expedient manner. Often the very people who were most disparaging of him during his drinking days will be his warmest supporters and admirers, once he has convinced them that he has stopped for good and all.

But the recognition and appreciation of friends and the discovery of a suitable occupation take time, so the former inebriate must have patience. A certain price has to be paid for his past stupidity and weakness, though in most cases it is not nearly so large as it might have been; and it is at least insignificant compared to the disaster that awaits him if he persists in seeking the impossible—that is, adaptation to life through the medium of drink.

Therefore, let him who feels that he is lost in an impenetrable maze pause a moment to reflect. Disaster awaits him if he continues in his present way of living. He cannot standstill, as he has a driving force within which will compel him to move in one direction or another. The way out, which many men have found to their everlasting satisfaction, lies open to him. It might be worth his while to seek for it.

Much has been made in this book of the desirability of undertaking the treatment only with those who clearly recognize the seriousness of their problem and who sincerely wish to do everything in their power to overcome the habit. This is essentially true, and the cases where the work can be started with a reasonable prognosis of success should be selected with some discrimination. However, there is this much to be said for those who at first refuse to see "the light of day" of their own accord. They are sometimes interested in an academic discussion of the subject, and it happens every so often that these academic discussions, without being in the least evangelical or proselyting, induce the alcoholic to investigate the situation more thoroughly. He may lose a few weeks of drinking, but he may decide that, after all, life holds too much to spend it under the influence of what has become for him a pernicious drug.

Summary

For the sake of those who wish to keep my argument in mind, I have summarized below the salient points in my exposition.

Those Whom Alcohol Poisons

An abnormal drinker is either a man who habitually behaves in an asocial, i.e. dangerous or disgusting manner, when under the influence of liquor, even though the time spent in this condition be restricted to reasonable limits; or one who, unlike his normal drinking friends, is unable or unwilling to face a return to reality. For these people a night's sleep is only a particularly long interval of abstention. This type is the true alcoholic. Sometimes both these characteristics of abnormal drinking are present in the same man. If not, the missing one is apt to be latent.

The Genesis Of The Habit

An individual becomes an alcoholic for three main

reasons:

1. As a result of inheritance he possesses a nervous system which is non-resistant to alcohol, (in no sense is a direct craving transmitted from parent to offspring.)

2. By reason of his early environment. Through the ignorance of his parents or from their own nervous constitution the alcoholic was either spoiled or neglected. He was not brought up to face the world courageously. He is lacking in self-reliance no matter how physically brave he may be or how bold he may appear on the surface. Psychologically he is unable to stand on his own two feet. As a result of this he unconsciously craves a stimulant-narcotic.

3. Because of the effects of his later environment. That is to say, school, college, economic and social competition, marriage, and, for one generation at least, the World War.

To Whom Re-education Is Applicable

Scientific treatment for the eradication of the drink habit can be successfully applied to sane men who have come to realize that drink has definitely disintegrated them to a point where they are no longer able to control themselves, but who would sincerely like to eliminate the habit if they could be shown how to do so.

The Treatment

The treatment consists in instructing a man how to train his mind so that he carries out a sustained course of conduct consistent with the theories of his most mature intellectual self, how to form new habits and stick to them, and conversely how to eliminate the unsatisfactory method of trying to adapt himself to his environment through the medium of alcohol. The reeducation is comprised of the following steps:

1. A mental analysis is made wherein the drinker learns that certain actions and systems of thinking, past as well as present, have directed him on the unfortunate course he has been pursuing, by creating doubts, fears, and conflicts. When these are removed his energy is free to take up more interesting and constructive occupations.

2. Various factors contribute to an abnormal state of tension which drink temporarily releases, only to aggravate it in the long run. This tension can be permanently removed by learning formal

relaxation and suggestion.

3. The unconscious mind can be influenced by suggestion so that it cooperates with the conscious to bring about a consistent, intelligent course of action.

4. Actions (where they are not mere reflexes) are the direct result of thoughts. Experience has proved over and over again that thoughts can be definitely controlled and directed when it seems desirable to do so.

5. As the body and mind are indivisible parts of the same organism, the mind is naturally much more efficient in the vigorous execution of new ideas if it is functioning in a sound body. To this end the elements of a normal, healthy hygiene should be followed. If there is any actual or suspected disability it should be attended to by a competent physician.

6. The alcoholic is to a large extent demoralized and disintegrated. To overcome this condition a direct attack must be made on the small habits of daily inefficiency. Alcohol is too strong an enemy to fight with untrained forces. To this end

living by a self-made and self-imposed schedule will accomplish three very important results: (a) The individual is continuously occupied; (b) he is conscious that he is doing something concrete about his problem (in contrast to mere intellectualizing); (c) he trains himself constantly in minor ways to obey his own commands. This develops an ability to say "Yes" when he means "Yes," and "No" when he means "No."

7. Various unexpected pitfalls into which people have previously slipped are carefully explained so that the drinker is forewarned and forearmed as much as possible against the future.

8. Some means of self-expression, some outlet or hobby to satisfy the urge to create, some means of absorbing the will-to-power must be energetically sought. The mind cannot dwell on the subject of not drinking all the time, important as it may be. It must be diverted, intrigued, and, if possible, inspired. This does not always happen until the cure is completed, but if it can take place earlier it is a great assistance to rapid recovery.

9. The individual is only an inferior person as

long as he continues to drink. The same driving force that has brought disintegration, if given a chance under conditions of sobriety, will carry him beyond the level of achievement attained by his average contemporary. He has an energy within which must be utilized constructively or it will destroy him.

What Dr. Milton Harrington says of people with strong instinctive tendencies seems to be equally applicable to alcoholics. Instinctive tendencies, he says, "drive some upward to success, while in others, who are unable to direct them into satisfactory channels, they are dammed up, find outlet in unhealthy ways, and so, instead of doing useful work, react on the mind to distort and destroy it."

—THE END—

.

Richard R. Peabody
1892—1936

Richard R. Peabody was afflicted with alcoholism in young adulthood, which was exacerbated by his wartime experiences. He had served as a Captain in the United States Army's 15th Field Artillery, 2nd Division, AEF, during World War I. His disease led to the disolution of his marriage. He became a disciple of the Emmanuel Movement, named for Boston's Emmanuel Church where clergy and lay practitioners reported success in treating alcoholics. He wrote "The Common Sense of Drinking," published by Little Brown in 1931, and reprinted in 1933, in which he was the first to state there was no cure for alcoholism. The book was a best seller and had a major influence on Alcoholics Anonymous founder Bill Wilson. Peabody continued to treat alcoholics though he was neither a medical professional nor a psychologist.